AFTER STEPHEN
From Hurting to Healed

A mother asks, "What do I do with the rest of my life?"

Cover Design	Linda Starkweather
	Kalamazoo, Michigan
	Louis W. Hands
	Photo-Expressionism Studio
	Kalamazoo, Michigan
Portrait Sketch	Parks H. Stephenson, USN
Typography	Sue Janes
	Kalamazoo, Michigan
Printing and Binding	Ihling Bros. Everard Co.
	Kalamazoo, Michigan

Order From	—ana Publishing
	Post Office Box 625
	Kalamazoo, Michigan 49005

After Stephen

From Hurting to Healed

Norma R. Lantz

*A bird does not sing because he has an answer
He sings because he has a song.* CHINESE PROVERB

-aP
—ana Publishing
Kalamazoo, Michigan

AFTER STEPHEN
From Hurting to Healed

Copyright © 1987 by Norma R. Lantz

All rights reserved. No part of this book may be reproduced or utilized in any form or by any means, electronic or mechanical, including photocopying, recording or by any information storage and retrieval system, without permission in writing from the Publisher.

Library of Congress Catalog Card Number 87-70625
ISBN 0-942419-00-6
Printed in the United States of America

—ana Publishing
Post Office Box 625
Kalamazoo, Michigan 49005

FIRST EDITION

*To Renée, whose faith in me never falters,
whose love for me made possible this book.*

With love and gratitude for these who have walked beside me, caught me when I slipped and equipped me for this leg of my journey, especially Mother and Dad, Mel and Valeri, Jackie; Eunice, Paula; Bart, Beth, Brian and their families; ministers and other friends unnamed; and Stephen.

And with appreciation to:

Francis R. Donovan, Rear Admiral, United States Navy
Lt. Col. R.J.M. Engler, M.D., Asst. Chief of Allergy and Immunology
   Walter Reed Army Medical Center
Vice Admiral William P. Lawrence, United States Navy
Scott Loveridge
Jack Moss, *Kalamazoo Gazette*
Lt. Col. and Mrs. E.W. Nettles, Retired, U.S. Army
Lt. Parks H. Stephenson, United States Navy
Dr. Hoover Rupert, United Methodist Church
Kit Smith and Giedré Ambrozaitis
Michael Timpe

Foreword

Now these are the laws of the Navy.
Unwritten and varied they be,
And he who is wise will observe them.
Going down in his ship to the sea.
ADMIRAL R.A. HOPWOOD RN

Midshipman Stephen Lantz and I had a great deal in common. We both attended the United States Naval Academy. We were both naval officers. We both underwent a *plebe year*, the traditional rite of passage that every young midshipman must undergo in his quest to join the long blue line of seagoing officers who are the heart and soul of the United States Navy. During that year both Stephen and I, although separated by more than a score of years, memorized The Laws of the Navy. Plebes have always done so. Plebes will always do so, and there is a reason for it. These laws are valuable lessons set to verse years ago which are learned early in one's career and recalled over the years. I quote my favorite verse here. I commend the rest to the casual reader.

> On the strength of one link in the cable,
> Dependeth the might of the chain.
> Who knows when thou may'st be tested?
> So live that thou bearest the strain!

Bill Halsey waited until the twilight of his career to be tested and to bear the strain during his magnificent performance as a fighting Admiral in the far reaches of the Pacific in World War II. Vice Admiral Bill Lawrence, Superintendent of the United States Naval Academy during Stephen Lantz' student days, had his test as a middle grade officer and as a leader of men during more than six years as a prisoner of war in North Vietnam. For others the test and the strain came much earlier in life. My classmate, Lieutenant (junior grade) Guy Parsons, who I am confident manned his station until the very end in an attempt to save his ship, the *USS Thresher*, met the challenge as did other classmates who perished in brief, fierce actions in Vietnam, who performed magnificently when the call came.

Stephen Lantz did likewise. His challenge came even earlier, and he performed magnificently. Stephen came to the Naval Academy from a wonderful home. He brought with him all the attributes sought in a Naval officer. He embraced life at the Naval Academy completely, and he lived it fully. I came to know Stephen well after his illness was diagnosed, and I can recall marvelling at his positive attitude, his cheerfulness and his faith. I was with Stephen the night that he was called to his eternal home, and I can remember thinking at the time how well he had borne the strain. I regret that we were not able to have him in the Navy for a longer time, but he remains with us in the example he left with his classmates and all with whom he was associated.

As for me, I have yet to be fully tested. I pray that when my turn comes I will be able to respond as well as did young Stephen.

FRANCIS R. DONOVAN
Rear Admiral, U.S. Navy
Commander, Amphibious Group 3

Preface

*"Each one must find a quiet place
within his mind. . . ."* CALDWELL

Late evening I set apart time to read, correspond, create handicrafts, plan for tomorrow, reflect. After our son died, I focused on mourning.

Many in grief notice that daily they are plunged into a specific interval of acute sorrow, and I was no exception. Although my husband's corresponding period came near the dinner hour, he also shared mine. After a while he protested that he could not continue. Disturbed by our talks, he could not fall asleep soon afterward nor awaken rested. I understood. As a homemaker my work hours were more flexible than his, but now there was no one with whom to vent feelings late at night. Yet, my need remained, so I began writing to replace our dialogues.

In school, theme assignments had been ordeals; but I later kept sporadic accounts of vacations, insights and whimsies of our children, herb lore and craft ideas—facts and anecdotes I thought too valuable to entrust to memory.

Death bred fresh motivation to write. *Catastrophe* was the headline, *Grief* the byline, words the outpouring of emotion. Returned from the United States Naval Academy with Steve's personal effects, a blank, spiral notebook became my first journal: imagined letters to him, recollections of our family's past twenty-one years and his last twenty-one days, reconciliations with loss, prose and poetry contributed by friends and kept to console, to be read again and again.

Occasionally I scribbled thoughts on scraps of tear-streaked paper, later transferring them into my logs of our encounter with adversity, the support we gleaned from varied sources and the stability we eventually gained. Spanning more than two years, the mélange overflowed into three additional notebooks that were relegated to my desk drawer after I had healed.

When I allowed a friend to read selections several months after Stephen died, she commented that those in circumstances similar to ours might be comforted by them. Not my nature to reveal intimacies to any but family or a close friend, I rejected her inference. "My husband and daughter haven't even read the journals."

"It's too soon," she continued, "but think about it later."

Later, the frequency of my journal entries ebbed as anguish also retreated. With my friend's persuasion and encouragement the idea for my book emerged: not an anatomy of our family tragedy, but a first-person image of grief, grief that could be caused by *any* severance from a relationship, by loss of health or financial security, by assault upon one's person, possessions or cherished others.

What does one do, how does one feel the day, the month, the year after a part of oneself has died? Not a clinical analysis nor a theological treatment, and not in retrospect, I had recorded feelings in their instants of eruption from a pit of hurting. Including excerpts from the journals written *After Stephen,* earlier jottings and moments culled from the diaries of memory, my story depicts our lives before and after the death of a son and brother. But it is offered to anyone who, in the throes of crisis, is certain to entreat as I had, *What do I do with the rest of my life?* NRL

Contents

Foreword ix
Preface xi
Without Warning 1
Thumbs Up! 5
Au Revoir, Étienne 23
Summer 37
Autumn 59
Winter 73
Spring 95
The Second Mile 109
Postscripts 137
The Physician's Review 141
Notes 155
References 157

Without Warning

"I know not what the future hath. . . ." WHITTIER

January 13 concluded the festive weeks of my favorite holiday. My husband Mel, our daughter Valeri and I drove to the airport with our son Stephen and his fiancée Paula where they boarded a flight to Washington, D.C. Reluctant to see them go, I knew how keenly Steve anticipated resuming his activities as a third-year midshipman at the United States Naval Academy. I had puzzled over a slight lethargy in him that Christmas leave, but dismissed it as a symptom of his annual December cold that had come home, too.

Later that month Steve called to say he had been discharged from a five-day stay in the infirmary. Admitted with moderately severe back and leg pains, he blamed a shower room fall incurred in November. Bed rest enabled his return to classes and now he was "feeling good."

February 15 brought further assurance by mail. "Leg and hip are feeling great. We [the USNA Drum and Bugle Corps] leave tomorrow for Mardi Gras . . . only two parades to march, each five miles long. We are the lead unit in both." Afterward he reported that a third five-miler had been added to their New Orleans' appearance. High energy restored.

The following month we received a call from Paula's mother. After becoming ill at their home during spring break, Steve was hospitalized, in isolation at Andrews Air Force Base, with suspected infectious hepatitis.

March 15 he wrote: "Well, contrary to popular belief, you do still have a son at Annapolis who does occasionally write letters, and who is alive and feeling fine.

"This was not much of a leave for me. I didn't feel well the three days I was at Paula's house and they convinced me to go for a checkup. Came here because it was closer than Bethesda. Today is my seventh day and I'm about to go batty. I can bring you up-to-date.

"The main problem is my white blood count which should be between 4,000 and 12,000 cells per cc. Mine was 1200 yesterday morning and has been around that since I got here. Three things could be causing the low count: an enlarged spleen which eats up white cells, the hepatitis virus is maintaining a depressed count, or the disease has shut off my bone marrow manufacture. I had a liver-spleen scan using a radioactive trace element yesterday and, depending on this morning's white count, will probably have a bone marrow tap, but that's not for sure, yet."

Including three additional pages of plans for future activities, Steve concluded: "So, that in a nutshell (a very large nutshell) is what has happened to me since my last letter. You all sound very busy as usual. I'll be busy, too, if I ever get outta here. Only 8 weeks and 40 school days until finals! Take care all. Much love." This was his last letter to us.

Steve remained quarantined until the white blood cells

reached the low-normal range, about 4800, and was discharged from the hospital to assume a regular schedule. Later we learned that a checkup and repeat bone marrow tap had been slated in three to four weeks.

During one telephone call I inquired, "How many other Mids got infectious hepatitis?"

"None."

A small weight pulled down a corner of my mind. Suspicious of a single case within an institution, I asked myself, *What, then?*

April 23. Near dinnertime, the phone rang. "Hi mom. Guess where I am again."

"In the hospital." Mel dashed to the extension downstairs as Val listened with me. "Why?" I asked.

"I was admitted this morning to Emergency at Bethesda."

"What's wrong, Sweetie?"

"They don't know for sure. My back and legs are giving me fits. I've been in excruciating pain off and on for two days. I practically had to be carried in here. It might be Hodgkin's. They have to run tests."

"Hodgkin's," I said. "I've forgotten what that is."

"I don't remember either."

"We'll come. Do you want us to come?"

"No need to right away. There's nothing going on here for three or four days except a lot of tests. Come later if you want." Steve knew we had returned two days earlier from a spring vacation.

"Are you sure? Well, we'll see. Who's your doctor there? At any rate, we'll keep in touch every day. Call again tomorrow night, around the same time if you can, so Dad will be here." We hung up stunned, worried, crying.

Telephoning our physician the next day to recap Steve's physical anomalies since Christmas elicited his terse comment: "If I were you, I'd go — now."

Late afternoon Steve's doctor at Bethesda answered the message I had left that morning. "I've been waiting for more test results before I returned your call. Your son is very ill. We aren't certain of a diagnosis at this time."

"We have just returned from a vacation. Would it be all right if we came on the weekend?"

Silence. "This appears to be quite serious. Steve has much ahead of him, painful procedures. He'll need us, his family and himself working as a team to get through it. If you can, come sooner."

"We'll be there tomorrow." As I replaced the receiver, the weight increased. The calendar beside the telephone marked tomorrow, April 25.

May 13 was Mother's Day. At 11:50 p.m., four months from his leave-taking at the airport and only three weeks from admission, critically ill, to Bethesda Naval Hospital, Stephen died of acute lymphoblastic lymphoma.

Thumbs Up!

*"When duty whispers low, Thou must,
The youth replies, I can."* EMERSON

Stunned, I automatically replaced the receiver after Stephen's first call from Bethesda. Mel came upstairs from the extension phone. "What in the world is all this about, do you suppose?" he asked. In the living room Valeri cried silently.

"What's the matter, Sweetie?"

"Brother's got cancer," was her choked reply.

"Is that what Hodgkin's is? How do you know?" I asked.

"I just read a magazine article about cancer and children."

"Oh, the one in *Saturday Review*? I saw that, but I haven't had time to read it yet. Where is it?" Pawing through papers and periodicals under the coffee table, we located the report which I read aloud to our tiny, worried group. The enormity of Steve's illness began to surface, but we thought the prognosis was far from hopeless. Breakthroughs in cancer research occur regularly. Many cancers are arrested, even cured if detected early. Yesterday's deaths may be today's remissions, tomorrow's recoveries. Hodgkin's is no exception.

Moreover, Stephen's health record had been good, an occasional bronchial cold his most serious ailment. Physically eligible for the Naval Academy, he had maintained a vigorous activity level. Although the forecast now appeared less intimidating, we decided to leave for Maryland by the weekend. After hearing urgency in conversations with our doctor and Steve's, we advanced our departure plans. That night I heard the clock chime each half-hour until the first weak rays of day backlighted the window.

Between washer-dryer summonses the next afternoon, I collapsed on the sofa. Despite fatigue, my mind ricocheted from one unrelated question to another. What clothes shall I pack? It's getting hot in Maryland. How long will we be there? What kind of Hell is entrenched in Stephen's body? Who else should we notify of his problem? When did this horrendous thing begin? What appointments have to be cancelled? The school year is ending. Will Valeri be able to complete assignments in time for finals? And what of his classes? The torrent subsided and I dozed. . . . Beneath the stained-glass window and before the carved, walnut altar of our church was a flag-draped casket. In a front pew sat Mel, Valeri and I. . . .

Pulses pounding, I sprang to my feet. "Why am I thinking these morbid thoughts?" I angrily demanded of the air as I strode to the kitchen for a cup of coffee. Ten minutes had elapsed since I lay down. The dryer buzzer had not yet sounded its alarm, nor were my questions and alarm answered.

As prearranged, Stephen phoned that afternoon to update his condition. Although now we could identify Hodgkin's disease, we avoided broaching the subject. However, before the conversation concluded, he commented, "By the way, I found out what Hodgkin's is. Do you know?"

"Yes," we quietly responded, "and we've also spoken with your doctor. We'll be there late tomorrow afternoon." We could not say more and Steve did not protest our imminent arrival.

At dinner we discussed the trip. The car had been serviced, luggage packed, parents and a few friends had been called, work and school schedules revised. To minimize delays we packed a lunch. "We're ready, so let's leave tonight!"

"No, we're too tired. It's nearly a twelve hour drive without any stops, and we didn't get much sleep last night."

"Well, we'll not sleep tonight either."

"I know, but at least we can rest until morning. I, for one, want to get there." I feared stress could collect its toll on an interstate.

Shortly before 4:00 a.m. I made one more restless turn in bed and Mel tossed in reply. Simultaneously we whispered, "Are you asleep?"

"No, shall we get ready to go now?"

"Why not, we're not sleeping anyway." Valeri was roused, and within the hour we were en route.

Mel and I drove in two-hour shifts. Who recalls what uncertainties careened around the convolutions of our brains? No banter. No anticipation of a dip in the motel pool at the conclusion of this trip. Each was submerged in private worry or mental anesthesia. Yesterday's dream focused and blurred; however, I did not share the incident nor the growing premonition that it was not just a bad dream, but a revelation. I saw no reason to add unfounded pessimism to an already depressed scenario.

As scenes flickered by the car window, I stared blankly at the spring-clad fields and mountainsides, progressions of towns and clones of cars. What traumas did their occupants also face today?

Isolated remarks were repeated to encourage, to convince. "Stephen is young and healthy, so that's in his favor."

"There was the fall in November, but that surely has no bearing on this."

"It could have caused the back and leg pains, though."

"He was fine at Christmas, maybe a little lower on energy than usual."

"Oh, Brother always crashes the first week he's home."

"They're discovering new cancer treatments every day."

"He surely couldn't be in a better hospital. The President and scads of important people go to Bethesda for treatment, so he'll have the best." We hoped the Naval Academy would not hastily revise Steve's future, for a discharge would devastate his morale. Our Olds made few stops, our minds none.

Exiting a final cloverleaf during afternoon rush hour traffic, we were impatient to confront the alien which had invaded the body of our Stephen. A short ride at a snail's pace brought us to the sloped hospital driveway. Crowding the building and parking lots were barricades and construction equipment, appurtenances to expansion of the facility. To one side lay the heliport. A central tower of rooms dominating the structure was like a windowed monolith casting long shadows across the grounds, and which would project brooding foreshadows across my mind as we entered and left the next seventeen days.

An elevator whisked us to the fifteenth floor. Near the nurses' station a white-coated woman conversed intensely by telephone. Instinctively I knew her to be the physician with whom I had spoken, and minutes later we were introduced to Dr. Engler. She deferred most of our questions until the staff meeting, scheduled pending our arrival. The rapidity of our assimilation into the medical team impressed us.

Perhaps we had expected worse. Our first impression as we entered Steve's room was that he appeared ill, but not critical. He described the pain that laid siege to this back and legs, making imperative his admittance to Emergency two days earlier; and he added details to symptoms and treatment previously recounted in letters and telephone chats. "I've cussed 'n discussed and 'peated 'n repeated all this stuff so many times, I'm blue in the face!"

The conversation shifted to our recent vacation in South Carolina. A military history buff, Stephen regaled us with the Civil War chronicles of the area and of the World War II carrier *Yorktown* moored there, chiding me when I, presuming a conclusion, interrupted him. I thought it more essential to be fully briefed with health data than sagas before our initial appointment with his doctors.

Mel, Valeri and I cannot recall how many were at the consultation, but they outnumbered us, their count increasing in direct proportion to the number of days that followed and the complications that arose. It would become a large team.

On a small poster affixed to the door of his hospital room, Steve had caricatured the teams at Andrews Base hospital with stick figures and penned satire.

This is the medical team. The team supports the belief that more heads are better than one. It has something to do with Jung's collective unconscious, I believe.

Dr. A is the team leader. She was made team leader because she has the coldest hands.

Dr. B is a zoomie. [Midshipmen's slang for graduate or student of the Air Force Academy] He spent four years at the government-funded playground in Colorado Springs. He has a moustache because they wouldn't let him have one at the playground.

Dr. C always looks like he walked out of surgery. Actually Dr. C hates to wear a uniform and the surgical T-shirt is more comfortable. He's no dummy!

Dr. D is the model physician. He strives to see his patients every day, always catching them in the john or shower. He does his best to encourage them: 'Let's sit around and watch your white count bottom out,' and he instills confidence: 'I have absolutely no idea what you have or when you'll be out of here!'

Dr. E has narrow, shifty eyes, but he seems nice. Perhaps now is the time to normalize relations with Dr. E.

This is a team, too, similar to the other one pictured. Note: neither team plays in the Super Bowl or World Series.

A is the team leader. Her hands are not cold; but with a frame like that, what else could she be!

B and C are clowns like Mutt and Jeff. Actually they kind of look like Mutt and Jeff.

D is the straight man (woman) for this team because I can't think of anything funny to say about her.

E spends more time with her car than with sick people. Can you blame her? She has discovered the ultimate solution to the energy problem—a car that weighs less than 2 lbs. It says so right on the side of the car: 24 oz.

F was the first person to discover my illness. He is the reason I am stuck here. He is not long for this world.

At the Bethesda physicians' meeting with Mel, Valeri and me, introductions preceeded their overview of the extent of Stephen's disease, current testing and tentative diagnosis: a lymphoma.

"Hodgkin's?"

"No, another type. We are unable to make a positive identification at this point, but it is very serious."

"Which means . . . ?"

"The disease is treatable, possibly curable, probably not, although it's too soon to say. We'll work for remission first."

Replies to further questions were factual but the tenor of the comments was guarded.

"What is the prognosis?"

"If he achieves remission, he can expect to lead a normal life, for awhile."

If. For awhile. "For how long?" I asked.

Pause. "Of course, we have no reason to believe he won't attain remission, once the correct chemotherapy is introduced. He's young and appears to have a good health record."

Just as we had presumed, but I persisted. "How many years might he have—ten, fifteen, more, less—do you have any idea?"

"We hesitate to make predictions. Naturally we cannot say for certain. At first we'd hoped for that many, but progression of the disease has been swift and severe."

Gently, then, one offered, "Three to five, seven at the outside." Stupefaction. Dear God. So soon. An A-bomb has exploded inside him.

The following morning Valeri and I entered the hospital through a rear door. Struggling to orient ourselves, we were addressed by a doctor we had met briefly the previous afternoon. "May I be of assistance, Mrs. Lantz?"

As we continued to the elevator I remarked, "Isn't it amazing that in this enormous hospital they know our name already? I certainly don't remember his."

"I wonder why they know us so well already," Val observed.

As the days multiplied, so did the numbers of those who recognized us and tended our needs even beyond normal, vocational responsibilities. That first morning we met another Steve, a lieutenant j.g. USNR and one of Stephen's nurses. Was their common name the link which quickly expanded a medical relationship into a family friendship? His cheerful countenance and steady companionship buoyed us during countless duty and off-duty hours.

Disease strikes. But as the days evolved, we witnessed a merciless assault. Lymph nodes in Stephen's neck and back swelled to resemble implanted ping-pong balls. His midsection became grossly distended. The skin on his legs was taut with edema, painful to the slightest touch. Supplementary oxygen eased breathing which had become labored. Extended phone conversations cheered but brought weariness. Dragging the intravenous stand and its pendulous paraphernalia from bedside to bathroom only six feet away exhausted him.

Nonetheless, his attitude was positive. "I know I can finish school if they'll let me. I heard about one midshipman with leukemia who served for eighteen months after he was commissioned, before he was discharged," he remarked one day.

No one asked, "What then?"

The Naval Academy confirmed that he could continue his studies, tutors provided if necessary, whenever he became sufficiently recovered. So he requested books and assignments. Friends braced him with food, flowers and gifts, prayers, sketches, cartoons and messages. "Like good wine and blue jeans, time does good things to friendships. Together we can whip anything, so if you need strength, use ours." The mother of one of Stephen's roommates at the Academy sent a medal of special significance, one commemorating Elizabeth Ann Seton,[A] that had been blessed by Pope John Paul II. Each said in every way she or he knew, "Thumbs up!" which also became a sign he and I exchanged each time I left his room.

Continued procedures, tests and biopsies led to no conclusive diagnosis. Chemotherapy was initiated less than twenty-four hours after our arrival. "We dare not wait longer," reported Dr. Engler.

We dared not ask, "Why?"

While awaiting the effects of the therapy, we assessed future plans. If Stephen's condition improved, Mel and Valeri would drive home to resume their schedules, return in two to three weeks and commute in that routine until Steve was discharged. Temporarily housed at the base motel, we had been provided a rental list of private lodgings. I would move to a sleeping room before their departure.

The weekend brought him stability and alleviation of some symptoms. Tuesday evening we transferred my luggage, then dined at the home of friends. It was past visiting hours when we returned to the hospital for our usual goodnight visit. During our absence dramatic deterioration had occurred. Head cradled in arms akimbo on the table that supported him, Stephen slumped, gasping for breath. Lung congestion had heightened and his subsequent transfer to the ICU (intensive care unit) would facilitate monitoring.

Despite reassurance from the floor staff that this was more precautionary than cause for alarm, we were not convinced and tabled the next morning's trip. We retrieved my possessions, but the landlady graciously offered to hold the room for a later arrival. "Things like this happen. You'll be along soon," said she who knew from experience.

The chronology of events and procedures that followed his relocation in the ICU is lost to exact recall, but we became intimate with two words, *waiting* and *room*. While we waited though, physicians paused to answer questions, relay lab findings or to report from medical conclaves almost as quickly as they ended. The medical, Naval, volunteer and civilian hospital staffs did not ignore, omit, nor merely tolerate us. We did not wait nor feel alone. While caring *about* coupled with caring *for* still may not cure, I believe they may have comparable impact on coping.

"It isn't working, is it? The chemo isn't helping," Valeri commented one morning as we crossed the base grounds.

"What makes you think that?"

"Well, they said he would be sick from it and his hair would fall out. That's not happening, so I didn't think it was working on the cancer either."

"I see what you mean. They're giving an anti-nausea drug to counteract that symptom," I explained, "and I'm not sure that hair loss still won't occur. I don't think that happens so soon. But," I added, "I'm afraid you're right. I don't think it's working either. Maybe it will just take more time, or maybe they'll have to try something else. Whatever—I hope there is a turnaround soon." There wasn't, and a second medical attack was launched.

The ICU staff had altered normal procedures for visitation and we rotated sitting with Steve. At first, if we remained longer than ten to fifteen minutes, he became agitated and indicated we should leave. One day I asked, "Are you tired?" He nodded yes. "Do you want to nap a bit?" Yes, again. Then I suggested, "Steve, you don't have to talk while we're here; it's too tiring. You don't need to entertain us. We've had many good talks before. Now we just want to be here, to sit by you. Do you think that would be OK?" He smiled with relief.

Thus, we related incidents and anecdotes, read notes from those unable to come, listened to soft music from the small radio on his pillow or exchanged comments with attendants. But often we just sat, hands touching. Outside the unit friends came to sit with those who waited their turn to sit awhile—and wait.

The blood bank dispatched the mobile unit to the Naval Academy and had to return a second day when more than eight hundred midshipmen and other personnel donors queued for hours. "Wow! That's a lot of vampire leave!" [Midshipmen's slang for leave granted for blood donation] "I can't believe they'd do that for me," was Steve's disbelief on hearing the statistics. But the response was not oversized for the demands of his body that became like the victim of a voracious vampire.

Other blood cell therapy was initiated. Through Pheresis[B] Mel, Valeri and I donated white blood cells to boost his critically low count which now was incapable of fighting infection, and platelets that normally assist clotting but were being destroyed by chemotherapy. Platelet reduction had precipitated internal hemorrhages of his alimentary canal. Each of us donated twice, but the procedure was abandoned for lack of positive response to our white cells. Platelets and red cells were furnished by continuous transfusions from the blood bank.

Stephen permitted an open-lung biopsy when the cause of continued respiratory problems could not be identified: infection, fluid accumulation, cancer cells or multiple suspects. We met the thoracic surgeon as he emerged from operating.

"How is he? How did the surgery go?" How the devil does one ask intelligent, leading questions of doctors?

Another predictable pause. "Oh, he came through the surgery quite well, very strong, no complications." The specialist yielded detailing of his probe to another.

Tentative travel was twice aborted when respiratory complications stormed again. This time we were summoned from the motel at midnight and advised to remain in the ICU waiting room until Stephen was out of danger. Near 6:00 a.m. we could quit our vigil on the recliners, but he had quit breathing without the aid of a permanent respirator, a heartbreaking development that also terminated oral food ingestion and speech.

Steve had been a garrulous extrovert. Now that tubes muted him, communication became an assortment of signs and mimes, penciled notes, gestures and postures, mouthing and spelling words on a small alphabet board devised by a staff person, or listening and touching, according to the moment.

Yet, a lone gesture can be totally expressive. Once as a corpsman prepared to serve the visibly unappetizing protein gruel through the oral tube, he joshed, "OK, Steve, here comes your T-bone steak!"

The day had been humorless; and lately we had refrained from mentioning food, for its absence dejected him. Valeri and I exchanged quick glances as we cried out inside, "Be quiet, you fool!" But, when the young man turned away, Steve dismissed him and his remark with a sharp jab of the finger, incongruous with his hand strapped to the intravenous arm board.

In an effort to control external bacteria, the frequency and duration of outside contacts were restricted and surgical masks became mandatory. While we did not object to the precautions, we felt frustrated by more limitations.

What thoughts and emotions crisscrossed his mind as he watched those black hands endlessly circle the large white-faced wall clock over the bed across the room? Each morning we inquired, "How was your night? Did you rest well?"

He usually responded, "No, I can't sleep long. They're always doing something to me." We could only nod in helpless understanding. Daily he asked, "When can I go back upstairs?"

Our answer never varied, "Soon, we hope, not today."

His depression concerned Dr. Engler. "He has been communicative, but lately he is very withdrawn. I fear if that continues, we may save the body but lose the mind. Have you noticed a change?" Yes, sometimes Stephen lay staring fixedly at the ceiling. What else could be expected from one bound to that environment? A comment from a nurse that another patient had lain there 89 days before returning to his room could scarcely conjure encouragement.

Surely he was trying to comprehend this "whole mess." Maybe he was concentrating on pain control and healing, maybe on the fly-leaf inscription of the New Testament left by a Naval Academy chaplain when he came to visit.

> "Lord, help me to remember that nothing is going to happen to me today that you and I can't handle."

Perhaps he struggled to reconcile himself to a possible future without all of us; perhaps composure came as he remembered a stanza which he had tucked into his Academy desk blotter.

> "So nigh is grandeur to our dust,
> So near is God to man,
> When duty whispers low, Thou must,
> The youth replies, I can."   RALPH WALDO EMERSON

Whatever the reason, we believed his dark moods to be less frequent than ours would have been under those circumstances. Afterward Mel said, "He was so brave."

At times I, too, felt quite removed from the situation, as if observing another's unfortunate episode: *This is not happening to our family.* Very often I mirrored his composure, a condition that I could only attribute to the prayers, thoughts and written communications from near and half a country away which constantly reminded, *You are not alone.*

Even if our lifestyles were disrupted, some normalcy continued. We read, wrote letters, shopped, conversed with visitors, commiserated with families of other ICU patients, telephoned progress (a real misnomer for reversal) reports, worked needlepoint, studied for exams, discovered restaurants and celebrated, no, *observed* two birthdays, Paula's and Valeri's.

Frequently we went to Steve's room in the tower to water plants, pick up mail or to bring a small necessity to the ICU. Each time, one of the custodial staff would inquire, "How is your son today?" She explained, "You know, the first time I went in to mop his floor, he asked me what my name was. He said, 'It looks like I'm going to be here awhile so I want to know the names of everyone who's gonna be doing something for me.' He's a fine young man. I sure hope he gets better soon, you tell him."

Awaiting the elevator one day, Mel and I noticed an information board which posted an in-house symposium concerning cancers of the circulatory system. Resource people from Johns Hopkins were mentioned. One of Steve's interns, also waiting, noted our interest in the sign and remarked, "I presented a paper on your son at one of those sessions."

"And. . . .?" And consultations with these and other experts, at the National Institute of Health and elsewhere, concluded alike: Every means known is being utilized to combat the disease.

"What do you propose if this doesn't work either?" I asked one oncologist after the second chemotherapy attack had begun. "Are there other alternatives?"

"We're not clear on that point. The bone marrow aspirates were inadequate and the types we're trying to identify are difficult to differentiate. We haven't even been able to locate the primary tumor source." Then he summarized: "Mrs. Lantz, we really don't know what we have here. There are hundreds of identifiable cancer cells, but one possibility we also must face is that Steve may have an undiscovered variant."

Stephen's body became a repository of IV's, tubes and catheters while blinking, pumping machines directed by challenged medical minds desperately struggled to save the life within— "heroic measures" the autopsy reported. But a firm beachhead was never established. He was a massive consumer of oxygen, blood cells, nutrients, medications, vitamins and minerals while being massively consumed.

Six months later my journal entry would sketch grim graphics of those days permanently etched in my mind.

One day Steve and I stared intensely into each other's eyes. "Am I dying?"

"There is nothing new on your charts to indicate that. In fact, there appears to be some improvement—at least you're more stable. The doctors have said nothing to lead me to believe so now. I have never lied to you. Do you believe me? See, I'm smiling." I hoped the wrinkles around my eyes would mirror those around my masked lips. We continued our eye probe for fleeting moments, but I finally broke concentration. I dared not raise his hopes too high. Did I also sense a lie?

*Subsequent indentations will denote my journal entries.

"He is so sick. It will take a miracle for him to get well," Mel commented as he and I walked to the hospital one morning.

"I think you're right," I replied; "and while I do believe in miracles, I guess I don't think one will happen this time."

I urged the landlady who continued to reserve my room to rent it. "Twice I've had to cancel. It's not fair to you. I can't give a definite day I'll be coming, or if I'll be coming."

"No, no," she insisted. "He'll get better, you'll see. My husband had some of these setbacks. You'll be coming later. I don't have anyone arriving for awhile anyway, so I can hold it for you."

Interrupting the unfolding tragedy were bright intermissions. Midshipmen arranged to "take Valeri away from this hospital scene" for dinner and a little party at the Officers' Club one evening. And the mother of an area classmate whom I had never met, and whose visit I missed, left me flowers in the ICU waiting room.

Regularly Stephen's company commander, her husband and dozens of shipmates came from Annapolis to visit. Paula and her family repeated the daily commuting, as during Steve's earlier hospital stays. On paper the letters of the word *miles* are easily rearranged to form the word *smile;* but round trips of eighty miles, often through heavy traffic, involved the restructuring of several lives for one resultant smile.

Darth Vader came to the hospital in a Trans Am. The imposing, black-garbed figure diminished his Naval companion in tropical whites, an unseemly pair.

"Here, here, you can't come in here!" protested an amazed ICU staff member as the two swung open the unit doors.

"Sure they can!" beamed Mel who met them as he was leaving. "Wouldn't it be possible for Steve to see them from a distance?" he coaxed.

"All right, but no closer than this," was their reluctant assignment to a spot near the nurses' station a few feet from his bed.

Rolling his head toward the sounds of commotion, Steve recognized the Halloween costume he and *Midshipman Vader* had fashioned from their cult-like engrossment with *Star Wars,* and grinned with delight at the visions of Good and Evil. The three exchanged thumbs up.

Darth and his escort then proceeded to Pediatrics where they were permitted to visit a group of ecstatic children, save one who cringed in a corner at the sight of the menacing character. "You should have seen the entourage that trailed those two through the halls!" Mel reported to Valeri and me who had missed the show. "It was larger than the group that followed the President!"

Leaving the hospital that previous weekend afternoon, Mel and I saw that the front steps were lined with brass (Naval officers). Small knots of civilians buzzed in the foyer under the scrutiny of tall, business-suited men who quietly conversed over walkie-talkies. A medical officer near us confirmed the rumor: the President was to arrive.

Mel dashed back to the ICU to bring Val to the reception area; and by the time they had returned, Jimmy Carter had alighted from the Marine helicopter. I could not stand with the family because the Secret Service already had ordered our growing assembly into a line, past which I assumed they also would sweep the President. Instead, he proceeded slowly, grasping each outstretched hand, murmuring a greeting. As our hands met, and even as I looked into the kind, smile-crinkled eyes of that former midshipman, I vacillated about referring to Stephen.

Steve had had opportunities to see and hear Mr. Carter; moreover, he was outspokenly critical of his politics. If I mentioned him and Jimmy Carter offered to visit the care unit, as I believed he would, might that action lend an air of finality to Stephen's situation? I dared not risk it.

Comparing notes afterward, Mel and I had reached the same decision; yet, I have since regretted mine. Respect for one's Commander-in-Chief and compassion for a person surely must be non-partisan.

One day as Val turned to leave Stephen's bedside, he signaled a medical corpsman and pointed at her retreating back. "My sister," he opened and closed his hands to count, "fifteen soon. Can you help?"

"Of course." On May 11 as Valeri sat in the ICU waiting room, a silk flower arrangement was delivered with its note: Happy Birthday Val from Brother via Ray. Steve wanted to surprise you. SURPRISE!

Corpsmen like this youth provided diligent care for body, boosted morale and fostered camaraderie within those austere, institutional walls. "They're great," Stephen remarked, and his sentiment was echoed.

"He's a great guy, in there fightin' every day. He's got a great sense of humor, too." I was glad they could exchange some; mine often went AWOL.

We saw his, though, in the small posters he had created during the earlier hospitalization, one describing the medical teams and another portraying his own military life and the mild rivalry that exists among the service groups.

- *This is a Midshipman.*
- *Midshipmen go to the Naval Academy in Annapolis, Maryland.*
- *Midshipmen occur in nature in four varieties:*
  Plebes (Freshmen)
  Youngsters (Sophomores)
  Second Class (Juniors)
  First Class (Seniors).
- *Most Midshipmen are clean, odor-free and housebroken.*
- *Inside this room is a Midshipman. He is not typical. He is sick. Note: All doctors outrank this Midshipman.*
- *Most Midshipmen like to drink, eat and sleep. They usually only study the night before a big exam.*
- *Some Midshipmen like to study. They are called* Geeks *or* Nerds.
- *All Midshipmen are single. They are not permitted to marry.*
- *Many Midshipmen get married after graduation. Note: This one is spoken for; his roommates are not.*
- *A Midshipman's education is worth $90,000. Unfortunately they get it a nickel at a time.*
- *Midshipmen are not permitted to leave the Academy except on weekends and leave. Note: This Midshipman is in isolation during weekends and leave.*
- *Navy's football team is composed of Midshipmen. Every year we beat Army's and Air Force's teams. They are composed of Cadets.*
- *Midshipmen do not like to be called Cadets. Cadets are an inferior form of life.*
- *The* Washington Post *calls Midshipmen* Middies. Mids *hate the* Post.
- *The Midshipman inside is going nuts. This is not normal. He is sick.*
- *Any questions about Midshipmen, inquire within.*

However, questions concerning one Midshipman within the walls of Bethesda Naval Hospital were conspicuously unanswerable.

Another bright interlude came from a stranger in Bethesda. A friend of a friend of a friend from home shopped for gifts and delivered them to our lodging for Valeri's birthday! We never met, but after Stephen's death she replied to my note of appreciation. "I'd like to share with you a quotation from Goethe that has meant a great deal to me:

'I am fully convinced that the soul is indestructible and that its activity will continue throughout eternity. It is like the sun which to our eyes seems to set in the night, but it has in reality only gone to diffuse its light elsewhere!'"

She never knew her outreach would begin my new collection — not antique curios nor driftwood and seashells — not trinkets for our home, but a collage of writings to cushion the dolor.

Midway through Stephen's third week, clinical developments heralded the first time that medical staff expressed cautious optimism. "I feel more positive about his overall condition than I ever have. There seems to be a change for the better," one reported. I shared this good news with him.

"Your charts show improvement, and everyone is encouraged. If this trend continues, no doubt Dad and Val will go home for awhile to get caught up; but I'll stay. I already have a room. Sunday is Mother's Day, so they'll probably not leave until early next week." His eyes widened, almost with incredulity. "I know. Maybe you don't feel better yet, but the prognosis is definitely better. You still have a long row to hoe." He nodded agreement.

Saturday evening we rotated visits as usual; but as I rose to take my turn, Mel cautioned, "Steve is very quiet tonight. I wonder if something is wrong."

"Really? He seemed even stronger today. What could it be? Maybe he's overly tired."

"Maybe, but I wouldn't give him thumbs up tonight."

"Really?" I repeated, astounded, "Well . . . I'll see."

After a quick chat I, too, detected a subtle change.

"Goodnight, Son, have a good night and I'll see you tomorrow morning." As I turned to replace my mask in the bedside table drawer, there was a tug on my arm.

His eyes reminded me, "You forgot something," as he signed the familiar farewell.

"Oh, by all means!" I hastily responded in word and gesture but turned quickly away again. My throat ached and I did not want to try to explain my brimming eyes.

Prior to midnight we placed the customary final phone call of the day to the nurses' station at the ICU. To hear that Stephen's condition remained stable, or had slightly improved, relaxed better than any sleeping pill. "He appeared to be having difficulties so the Swan-Ganz catheter [used to monitor cardiorespiratory function] has been restored. It's just a precaution," was the report.

Puzzled, we asked each other, "Why is this necessary if his condition is improved?"

Au Revoir, Étienne

*"But wait, before he leaves,
Be sure he knows you love him."*
AUTHOR UNKNOWN

Grey crowned a Mother's Day dawn, but inside our motel Valeri and Mel tried to lighten the oppressive mood under which we awakened with a bottle of sparkling Burgundy from him and a summer handbag which Steve and she had conspired to have her select from a nearby shopping mall. Their card held two signatures, except both in her handwriting. To show Stephen their gift, I quickly transferred the contents of my old purse to the new.

As we left, Mel noted the ominous clouds. "We'd better take the car today."

"If you two don't mind," I suggested, "I'd like to skip chapel and sit with Stephen. Especially today."

"Fine," they agreed. "Then we'll go out for dinner later, if you'd like."

"That's OK only I had hoped we could make up a picnic and go for a hike in this beautiful park I discovered the other day; but that doesn't look possible now."

At the hospital entrance we went in opposite directions. On Sunday mornings the atmosphere was like that of a ship becalmed. The weekday bustle had subsided and, as yet, no one was waiting in the anteroom of the ICU when I opened the door and started toward a cluster of white coats. Rarely were medics' huddles good omens. The larger their group, the more somber their reports. Something inside knotted when I saw the grave faces that awaited me.

Dr. Engler came to walk beside me and grasped my hands. "I'm so sorry. I don't know what has happened. When I left yesterday, I had never felt more encouraged. They called me around 3:00 this morning. All Hell has broken loose. Infection is raging again, and the white cell count has fallen drastically. He's not responding to anything. We've had to reinsert the Swan-Ganz cath and increase the oxygen level to one hundred percent."

I nodded dumbly. "We knew about the catheter from our call last night. We wondered why."

"It was precautionary, unexplained changes . . . we're doing everything we know to do, but nothing seems to be working."

"Shall I call my husband and daughter from chapel? I decided to come here instead of going with them since it's Mother's Day."

"I know. No, he is critical, but he's stable again for the time." Now we had joined the discussion.

"Is there anything left?" I asked them.

"We can take him and all his tubes and machines down to radiation and give him a shot in each lung. We can try Pheresis again, put you all back on the machine for white cells."

"That wasn't successful before," I replied.

"No, and his fever spiked every time, but we could try again."

"That also means each of the family would have to be away from here for two or three hours." I stared intently into each doctor's eyes, some tear-filled. "Do you really believe that or anything else is going to work?"

Pause. "No."

"All right, then, I say 'no more'. I'll speak with my husband and daughter when they get here, but I think I know their answers. How much time are we talking about?"

"It's difficult to say. He cannot continue long at this oxygen level without irreversible brain damage, and he may soon lapse into coma. Maybe up to three days, but if I were you, I would say whatever you have to say to him today. I'm so sorry," Dr. Engler added. "I just don't know what to say to you except that sometimes the good die young, and *that* we can do nothing about." Then she inquired tenderly, "One thing more. No one else seems to have the guts to ask you, but will you permit an autopsy? We would like to study his cells."

"Yes, I'm sure it will be all right, but that will have to be a family decision, too." Then I paused. "He always wanted to serve his country. Maybe this is one way he'll be able to do it."

"It's all in God's hands, now," an oncologist commented.

"It always has been," I replied.

As I turned toward my dying son and our eyes met, Stephen and I knew this was goodbye. I told him that his dad and sister were at the Chapel and then asked if, in thought, he wanted to go home to church with me. "Maybe we can hear some words from Dr. Rupert to help us," I said as we joined hands to fervently repeat "The Lord's Prayer." Then he rested.

When he awoke, he jabbed the air as he had done when he asked to return to his tower room. "Do you want to go upstairs?" What would my answer be today? Negative nod, and he motioned again. "Ahh—you want to go home!" Affirmative smile. "And so you shall, my son, with us and God." But my voice choked on the last four words. I grabbed the alphabet board to spell them. As he followed my shaking finger, our eyes met again—his in peaceful acceptance, mine flowing like the drizzle that patterned the windows by his bed.

Meeting Valeri and Mel in the hall on their return from the service, I reiterated the physicians' deliberations and admitted, "It's no use—he's dying." We discussed and rejected last resort treatment proposals; we would remain a family of four as long as allowed. "Dr. Engler suggested we'd better tell him whatever we want, soon," I added.

What last words were spoken? Dr. Engler suggested the Twenty-third Psalm, but I was too agitated to recall all the phrases, learned and recited from childhood, without her prompting before we clustered around Steve's bed. What does one say to the dying for them to take? What do they say to us who remain? Long after, I found that morning's chapel bulletin with fitting words. Perhaps it was as well that our own spoke our hearts.

"You're the best brother anyone ever had."
"I love you."
"If I could trade places with you, I gladly would."
"I love you, too."
"You three mean more to me than life."

Indelible images disclosed in my journal would be written with a pen compelled by a mind that refused to forget.

I had to trust a strong handclasp to give Stephen faith when he pleaded with eyes and hands to help him conquer the myriad tubes and machines.

"Disconnect the plugs!" he commanded each and pointed accusingly as we tearfully refused.

"Stephen, you cannot ask your parents or your sister to do that," said Dr. Engler softly.

"Then you!" he stabbed the air.

"Nor me," she said.

"God will take care of that, Son," was all I could say.

He was hurt and angry at our refusal to help him escape. A promise made and broken? A lack of understanding? Confusion? No compassion to end his suffering? He surely thought these things, and rightly so, after our earlier affirmations.

In prior years our family had discussed dying, especially when extraordinary measures were taken to artificially prolong life without apparent regard to its quality. Indeed, in the bed opposite Stephen's lay a long-comatose patient without brain patterns on his monitor. Daily his spouse agonized over a lack of resolution, for they never had agreed upon a declaration of final intent. We, on the other hand, had mutually pledged that we would not encourage the use of machines merely to extend existence, and would request their removal. At that time, I may have been deluded by an oversimplified option, made when the family were even younger, in good health, and relating its application to my own possibly future condition. Now, during his terminal hours, even aware of Steve's prognosis, I met the dilemma of reality, moments of greatest tumult amid the entire three weeks.

And then he slept. When he awoke, he seemed at peace.

"Where's Mom—and Dad?" he asked Val who had not escaped with us to the outer corridor.

"They went to get a cup of coffee."

He nodded. "It's OK. Everything's going to be OK." His lips formed the statement of assuredness.

Did Stephen glimpse a corner of eternity? He seemed to know his time to leave would come soon, but first there were tasks to be done, goodbyes to be said. And as he said each one courageously and lovingly, he gave us strength.

Only Mel had the grit to solicit his consent to one heart splitting question, interment. "Son, since you have been very ill, your mother and I have had to think about decisions that might have to be made. We thought you might like to be buried at Arlington." Affirmative nod. "But then we also thought you might want to go home." Affirmative nod. "Do you want to go home first, and then come back to Arlington?" Enthusiastic approval.

Paula and her family arrived. By early afternoon other friends came from Annapolis and continued to appear throughout the day. "We heard Steve was worse. There was a rumor he might need more blood. We decided to come and see for ourselves. What happened? Can we do anything to help?"

"He's dying."

"Can we see him?"

We requested the suspension of masks and visitation limits. "No harm can come to him from outside now. Let him see these people." It was done and a steady procession stood by two's and three's to say *We're with you, Steve, for as long as we can be.*

"You're going to a better place than this, my friend," said an officer. "Say 'Hi' to Jesus for me."

Steve exchanged farewells with friends and salutes with his Naval commanders: *Bon Voyage, we'll meet again.*

On the radio John Denver sang a favorive, "Take me home, . . ." Valeri and I heard, our glances could but touch across his bed and we wept. And someone brought a tape recorder to play Steve's favorite tapes of Paula's ballads, and they quietly sang together.

Visitors left us to be alone as the long, yet too short day drew to its close. "What will happen when Brother dies?" asked Val apprehensively.

"What do you mean?"

"Will he be in a lot of pain, or thrash around, or what?" She had overheard someone discussing involuntary muscular activity which may accompany death.

"Oh, no, I'm quite sure he will just continue to sleep until his heart and brain functions stop. We'll know by the monitors, but . . ." I hesitated. What will happen when Stephen dies? I could not provide details for I had never seen anyone die, either.

"Is something the matter?" asked one of the physicians.

"Our daughter is nervous, unsure of what will actually happen when her brother dies." He nodded, said nothing to me, but put his arm around her shoulders as they stood near the bed, and gently explained so she would be unafraid.

The Deputy Commandant of Midshipmen spoke with me in the hall. "I hesitate to ask you, especially at this time, but there may not be a better one. What will you do with the ring?"

The Naval Academy class ring. I shook my head. No deliberations. So anticipated, Stephen's was at the jeweler's. Its selection had prompted a long-distance conference. "What stone should I get? I'd really like a black, star sapphire, but that costs a little more."

"Choose whatever you want. You didn't get a high school ring and this will be the most important one you'll ever own, aside from a wedding band."

After it arrived, Stephen proudly carried it in his pocket because it could not be worn before the conclusion of 2nd Class year. Mid-April he relinquished it for sizing, where it remained. It nearly became a topic for conversation one day while he was in the ICU; but when he rolled his eyes in despair, the subject was dropped. In retrospect, I believe he knew he would not wear it long, if ever.

Captain D— continued, "In the Naval Academy Museum is a memorial ring case. The first to die from each Academy class may be honored by the placement of his ring in the case, if the family agrees. I would be pleased to make the arrangements if you want to consider making the gift." Mel and Valeri endorsed the suggestion as appropriate, but Stephen was not consulted, for the end of the day was near. He did wear it once, however, as he lay at rest, at home.

During the discussion with Captain D— outside the ICU, I suddenly felt compelled to return. Mel and Valeri stood beside a slumbering Stephen. "Where have you been?" she asked. "We've been waiting for you."

Rejoining their vigil, I began to stroke Steve's brow. Rolling his head toward me, he forced open his eyelids. "It's Mom, good Buddy." Visually he hesitated. Then closing his eyes, he slowly turned back. Four pairs of hands touching, we awaited his impending departure. A few feet away, medical personnel quietly snapped to attention as he set sail for a new port, a larger assignment, just prior to midnight, 13 May.

> We walked through the main doors of the tall, somber, tower-spectre, Mel, Valeri and Steve (our friend and Navy nurse) after a grey day of rain and dismal hours. Overhead the stars winked as if to say, We're back, as if to lift the rain curtains which formed a backdrop for the thunderbeats of our fearful hearts and the lightning stabs of knowing that our son and brother lay silent there.
>
> The warm, moist air enveloped and insulated me against the mindfulness of cold walls, now silenced machines and disconnected tubes in one small cubicle of the ICU. Outside, the smells were pure and fragrant with blossoms, sharp contrast to the antiseptic whiffs which tried to soften the creeping stench of death—not actually detected, but sensed by us around Steve's bed and tasted deep down clenched gullets.
>
> "It feels so good," I said aloud, and thought, so good to be free of pain and fear, uncertainty. And I knew our Stephen knew these same truths as he soared home, somewhere, to God. And I knew and he knew Joy in the Morning. [c]

Next morning we awakened from exhausted sleep to tackle the particulars of a military burial with the Director of Decendent Affairs at the hospital and Steve's company commander. "I know two funerals may be very difficult for you," said the latter; "but because of final exams, none from here will be able to attend the one at your home, so I hope you will consider a memorial service at the Academy Chapel." In view of burial arrangements, her suggestion sounded reasonable to me. Could we feel any worse?

After making hospital rounds to acknowledge the medical efforts of several staff, we went to the fifteenth floor one final time to collect Stephen's belongings. Near a corner of the hall stood his friend the cleaning lady. Today, she made no inquiries as our glances met. She could but stand and weep silently, clutching her mop.

Forgotten for twelve days, but undisturbed in the bedside table drawer, lay Steve's billfold. Inside were a five dollar bill and thirteen ones, the fifth month, thirteenth day. For how long would those numbers recur to remind? The accumulated items would not fit into his suitcases, so many were packed in a giant, black plastic bag. On the crowded elevator, I bridled a desperate outburst to stares at our cumbersome baggage. "They belong to my dead son!"

During the fourteen-hour drive home, I pondered how Stephen will say *au revoir,* until we meet again, to those who had been with us via telephone reports, to some just returning from college, to others who will be shocked by the press releases, without warning. The memorial service at home will speak for him with favorite music, poetry and prayers.

Written in 1860 by a clergyman from the Church of England, after he had weathered a severe storm in the Mediterranean Sea, the Navy Hymn concludes each chapel service at the Academy. We who also have weathered a tempest need its message.

> "*Eternal Father, strong to save*
> *Whose arm hath bound the restless wave,*
> *Who bidd'st the mighty ocean deep*
> *Its own appointed limits keep;*
> *Oh, hear us when we cry to Thee. . . ."* WILLIAM WHITING

I liked to remember Steve as our Don Quixote, arms outstretched and perched atop the living room hassock, belting that lyrical idealism of quests. Selections from "Jonathon Livingston Seagull", "Christ the Lord is Risen Today" and Handel's "Hallelujah Chorus" completed the music, but I later wished I were bold enough to have suggested "Anchors Aweigh" and excerpts from Steve's album of the movie *Patton,* as pièces de résistance.

Found on a snip of paper in his wallet were stanzas from *The Eternal Goodness.*

> ". . . I know not what the future hath
> Of marvel or surprise,
> Assured alone that life and death
> His mercy underlies.
>
> "And if my heart and flesh are weak
> To bear an untried pain
> The bruised reed He will not break
> But strengthen and sustain. . . .
>
> "And so beside the silent sea
> I wait the muffled oar.
> No harm from Him can come to me
> On ocean or on shore.
>
> "I know not where his islands lift
> their fronded palms in air;
> I only know I cannot drift
> Beyond His love and care. . . ."
>
> JOHN GREENLEAF WHITTIER

With other petitions, we would pray one used as a family grace whenever Stephen was home.

> "Almighty Father, whose way is in the sea, whose paths are in the great waters, whose command is over all, and whose love never fails: Let me be aware of Your presence and obedient to Your will. Keep me true to my best self, guarding me against dishonesty in purpose and in deed, and helping me so to live that I can stand unashamed and unafraid before my shipmates, my loved ones and You. Protect those in whose love I live. Give me the will to do my very best and to accept my share of responsibilities with a strong heart and cheerful mind. Make me considerate of those entrusted to my leadership and faithful to the duties my country has entrusted to me. Let my uniform remind me daily of the traditions of the Service of which I am a part. If I am inclined to doubt, steady my faith; if I am tempted, make me strong to resist; if I should miss the mark, give me the courage to try again. Guide me with the light of truth and keep before me the life of Him by whose example and help I trust to obtain the answer to my prayer, Jesus Christ our Lord. Amen.   THE PRAYER OF A MIDSHIPMAN [1]

Condolements began to arrive before our return from Bethesda, not only from friends, but those from whom we had drifted apart, even from a stranger—a woman who had felt the death of a child. Words that detailed what we had lost gave comfort, in part contradicted the fact of loss. A letter from the Superintendent of the Naval Academy already waited.

> "Steve has been one of the outstanding members of the Class of 19—. His overall rank was 71 out of 970... recognized as a leader, having been selected as a Batallion Commander... included in both the Superintendent's and Dean's Lists... a member of perhaps the most outstanding Drum and Bugle Corps the Naval Academy has had. I know that you have lost a fine son. I want you to know that we are certain the United States Navy has suffered the loss of an exceptional midshipman and officer of great potential.

The sports editor of the local paper wrote that he "led by example and reflected the best in young people. The standards he set in a life cut short will prove an inspiration to other young people. That is his greatest legacy."

Friends and neighbors had mowed the lawn, cleaned and ordered the inside of the house which relieved that aspect of homecoming. We never could thank each who continued to say: You are not alone. We care. Sorrow isn't forever, love is; but you will need time to grieve, surrender the past, find peace with the living.

Beneath the stained-glass window and before the carved, walnut altar of our church was a flag-draped casket. In a front pew sat Mel, Valeri and I who, with others, heard the words of our minister.

> "Death has come suddenly and taken from our presence a young man on the threshold of his career—still seeing visions, dreaming dreams, planning plans. It has brought the end of

our dreams and hopes for this life. It seems so final. Yet, are we really separated from his life? His family will cherish experiences which have accumulated in their store of memories these twenty-one years. You, his schoolmates and friends remember your experiences. He has made a contribution in every life who has known him. Nothing can separate us from those experiences, those memories.

"Someone said of him, 'He touched people with care.' It reached into our lives and helped us know what love in human relationship is. Can you believe that the love Steve shared is lost now that death has taken his body? No death can rob us of his spirit.

"We cannot be separated from the purpose and direction which guided Steve's life. One who had known him since childhood said to me yesterday, 'I have never known a young man so strongly motivated. He knew where he wanted to go and was willing to pay the price to get there.' Such purpose and direction in a life can lead to bankruptcy, but not when coupled with moral standards. He was unashamedly one who believed in serving God and country.

"When death came, Steve was at peace. And his faith can bless us as we remember him. If this voice, now stilled, were again to speak for a moment, I wonder if he might say something like this:

*"If I should die and leave you here for awhile,
Be not like others, sore undone, who keep
Long vigil by the silent dust and weep.
For my sake turn again to life and smile,
Nerving thy heart and trembling hand to do
That which will comfort other souls than thine,
Complete these dear unfinished tasks of mine,
And I, perchance, may therein comfort you."*

AUTHOR UNKNOWN

Funeral ceremonies are for the survivors, not the deceased. Stephen's had spoken well about him. I hoped it also had been from him: *Goodbye, God be with you.*

The morning after the funeral, we drove to the airport to board Stephen on his last flight East. Under the watch of a Midshipman 1/c from his company, the plain, strapped box was lifted into the nose of a commercial airliner. Mel, Valeri and I stood outside the restricted runway area until take-off. "Why that's a casket, I think!" exclaimed a nearby voice. "A military casket, isn't it?" She had spied the uniformed escort.

With fingers clenched over chain links I heard me croak, "It is."

Two days later our mini-caravan of three family cars paralleled the plane's route, fourteen hours and miles of time to think and compose a thank you letter to the Brigade (student body) and their officers.

I included a concept that I also had shared with Stephen in the ICU. God might be compared with a weaver of rugs. As artist He designs and as craftsman He creates the intricate patterns of our lives which He views from the topside. Sometimes we see only the uglier, reverse side—without design, loose threads dangling—but the completed product is in accordance with His plan. I was to learn that simply repeating a philosophy of faith paled beside the effort of practice.

Despite the academic pressures of exam week, members of the 11th Company, together with officers and four chaplains compiled and conducted the moving, chapel service of personal witness and remembrance. Perhaps I should not have been surprised at similarities in music, scriptures and meditations between theirs and the one at home; but any apprehension I may have felt regarding plural funerals was dispelled by the solace I gained from each.

At Arlington National Cemetery, mourners paced behind the flag-draped caisson and riderless horse to a cadence set by the Drum and Bugle Corps, while reverberations of rumbles and shrieks issuing from Washington National Airport punctuated the graveside ceremonies. For the second time, I felt a moment of detachment: *I am not here.* An aunt who stood with us later mailed me a poem.

Forgive Me

"Forgive me if I do not cry
The day you die,
Streams at some seasons
Wind their way through country lanes of beauty
And are dry.

"The willow bends its head
To kiss the empty river bed
With the same caress it gave
When in its heyday it was full and high
Oh river know that I remember
The splashing laughing clatter
Of bubbling day in Spring
When everything was blossoming!

"Butterflies still hover
Down the rocky bed
And weeds grow strong and
Guard the pebbled way.
In this high noon of nothing
Which is death
Brave flags still wave
Cowslip-parsley, rag weed and sorrel
Shout to me
That Spring is on her way
Comfort, I am still too deaf to hear.

"Yet forgive me if I do not cry
The day you die
The simplest reason that I know
You said you'd rather have it so
And that I held my head serenely high
Remembering the love and glory that we knew.
Forgive me if I do not cry
The day you die . . .
Forgive me
If I do. . . ."[2]

We had watched Stephen in the Drum and Bugle Corps march with brio through the streets of Winchester, Virginia at the Apple Blossom Festival and across the football field in Philadelphia, at the Army-Navy game. Vicariously we had known their spirit, underscored in their music at Arlington which now undergirded our company.

> "When you walk through a storm
> Keep your chin up high,
> And don't be afraid of the dark.
> At the end of the storm is a golden sky
> And the sweet silver song of a lark.
> Walk on through the wind,
> Walk on through the rain,
> Tho' your dreams be tossed and blown,
> Walk on, walk on, with hope in your heart,
> And you'll never walk alone,
> You'll never walk alone!"[3]

Someone remarked that a few of the brasses' highest notes quavered at the conclusion, but we only heard their tribute to a shipmate. And the drifting notes of "Taps" serenaded *encore* all those in repose. Was it coincidental that the first recorded strains of music at the Officers' Club where we dined that evening were those of "The Impossible Dream"?

Au revoir, mes amis.

Summer

> "... and ever, as the summer goes,
> a deeper loss in losing thee!" VAN DYKE

The postlude to a tragic finale opened with the reprise of a numbing, fourteen-hour auto ride. No unanswered questions pertaining to Stephen's future, no ceremonies to mull, nothing to plan—save the remainder of our lives which now lacked a vital element. A family and future without him was incomprehensible. What would be the aftermath? My journals would accompany me through more than two years of ferment.

Losing a son or daughter must be like amputation. A part is destroyed forever. There are no transplants available, no regenerations. Although the part is removed, sensation remains. The part lives, it tingles, it pains. It throbs with feeling, but it is gone. Therapy begins. Re-education, adjustment, patience, perseverance, work, faith. How to live without the part? How to love? How to feel whole again when you're not? How long will it take?

Empty-hearted we unlocked the door of an empty house, but out minds were not devoid of the horror of the past thirty days. Sandwiched in the accumulated mail was notification of a package which Mel retrieved from the post office early the next morning.

Not inquisitive enough to note the sender's name on the mailer, I was totally unprepared for the visual impact of its contents: Stephen smiled at me from an 8 x 10 color photograph. Other pictures lay beneath. Although the sitting had been months earlier, we were unaware the prints, earmarked as Christmas and graduation gifts, would be sent home.

He had telephoned from the hospital at Andrews to discuss the proofs. "A smiling one or serious, with a cover (regulation cap) or without? There are lotsa possibilities."

Without a cover, I think" I suggested. "A serious expression would be appropriate for an officer, but smiling is more like you. How 'bout a small, dignified smile?"

"Yeah, that's kinda what I thought, and the nurses like those best, too."

"Everyone's so excited—little more than a year now until you're commissioned!"

For a long time I stared at the packet. It was as if Stephen had arrived ahead, to welcome us. I'm not sure he wasn't here. His eyes look different from other pictures, from Plebe year and the family portrait just taken in January. Eyes are the windows of our souls; his seem to look beyond.

Shortly thereafter a second package arrived, this from Bart Sparks, one of Stephen's first friends at the Academy. On the inside back cover of the monthly magazine published by the Brigade was a sketch of Steve drawn by the Co-Art Editor, Parks Stephenson, alias Darth Vader. The inscription read, "We would like to dedicate this issue of *The Log* to Stephen Lantz, a shipmate of ours. His sense of humor is the kind that keeps us going. The support of the Brigade is appreciated by everyone close to him." The postscript added, "We're going to miss you, Steve." A second unexpected item in Bart's parcel was a recording. In the background of the album cover a flag flies at half-mast, the picture having been taken during the official mourning of a government dignitary. Stephen stands in the foreground flagline of the 130 member Drum and Bugle Corps whose repertoire includes "You'll Never Walk Alone."

One Night I Had a Dream

"I dreamed I was walking along the beach with the Lord; across the sky flashed scenes from my life. For each scene I noticed two sets of footprints in the sand, one belonged to me, the Other to the Lord. When the last scene of my life flashed before us I looked back at the footprints in the sand. I noticed that many times along the path of my life, there was only one set of footprints. I also noticed that it happened at the very lowest and saddest times in my life. I questioned the Lord about it. 'Lord, you said that once I decided to follow You, You would walk with me all the way, but I noticed that during the troublesome times in my life, there is only one set of footprints. I don't understand why in times when I needed You most, You would leave.' The Lord replied, 'My precious child, I would never leave you during your times of trial and suffering. When you see only one set of footprints, it was then that I carried you.'" AUTHOR UNKNOWN

God has had to carry me so far these long weeks. There has been but one set of footprints in the sand. I see no end to this pattern.

I have never known grief—sorrow, not grief. Grief is more acute. No matter what befalls me henceforth, I shall never know greater grief, equal no doubt, but none greater. The first taste devastates. Through our tears we ask, "Why him?" No answers yet, just grief and more tears.

"In this sad world of ours sorrow comes to all . . .
it comes with bitterest agony . . .
Perfect relief is not possible, except with time.
You cannot now realize that you will never feel
better . . . and yet it is a mistake.
You are sure to be happy again.
To know this, which is certainly true,
Will make you some less miserable now.
I have had experience enough
to know what I say." ABRAHAM LINCOLN

Dared I equate my loss to that suffered by this President who, in his lifetime, faced the deaths of three sons and 600,000 of our country's sons in one catastrophic moment in history? Feelings were common to our tragedies, if not the circumstances.

A few days after our return from Arlington, a woman telephoned from the funeral home that had handled local arrangements.

> She identified herself as a counselor in grief who offered classes for the bereaved. "There are workshops available. If there is anything I can do, anyway we can help, please call." So, help is available when and if we need. Friend, we who grieve, need! Our problem is we don't always know if or when.
> I wanted to ask: Did you meet the planes that brought him home or took him back? We were there. Why are you a stranger's voice? Why didn't we meet you at the mortuary? Could you have begun to disperse your expertise earlier? We needed a compassionate face not tied to burial-business details to answer questions, or maybe simply to sit awhile, someone who might say, "You don't know me, but I am here to help you now or whenever you may call," and then wait in the wings for a cue. The newspaper ads for your course say class size is limited so we must enroll on time. Grief surely is neither limited nor timed. And the sessions are numbered. What if my grief has not abated by the end of four or five workshops?

What seemed insentience to my recovery readiness made me rebel against the counselor's curt, impersonal invitation. I did not want to be healed. Then was too soon for me to study grief and how to resume normal patterns of life. Later I never initiated a contact, nor did she call me again.

We did read about grief support from a friend who clipped an article describing The Compassionate Friends, a self-help organization offering bereavement assistance to parents who have lost a child. Ten stages of grief were explored: shock, intensified emotions, depression and loneliness, panic, guilt, anger, resistance, physical symptoms of distress, gradual hope, and a struggle to reaffirm reality. The theories had been expounded;

now we, too, would venture daily trials. In the months that followed, we would maneuver the steps, not necessarily in the order delineated, sometimes taking two or more simultaneously, and with pendulum swings of progress and regression that felt like running up the down escalator.

Members of the local chapter of Compassionate Friends contacted us with letters and calls, but apologized because the group was not meeting during the summer. Would that Death take a holiday!

Mel and I had begun writing to heal fractured sensibilities, I in the journal and he in a narrative about Bethesda. That the discourses lacked sophistication was inconsequential. The words mirrored turmoil within, one more compress to stanch tears gushing from a gaping hole of loss. He abandoned, then destroyed his effort after twenty-five pages. "I found it made me more morose," he explained. His high period of anguish came at the close of his workday when he ran Stephen's arthritic dog, Boots, in the neighborhood field.

"*The most exciting thing that ever happened to me was when I got my dog. He is black and tan, part cocker and springer spaniel. His tail is always wagging, and when we give him a bath it feels heavy. After supper he stays in the family room and sleeps on his rug; but when we watch TV, he hops up on the sofa and lays his head on my lap and feels nice and warm and safe. His name is Boots and I love him,*" Steve had written in a grade school autobiography.

Last summer when Boots was failing [in health] *I thought, If he should die, how hard it will be to tell Stephen that his beloved pet is gone. This summer I cry, How do you tell a pet his beloved master is dead?*

While Mel walked with Boots, he composed the single poem which escaped disposal in the round file.

"Stephen,
our beautiful son,
we laid you to rest at Arlington.
You are love
and joy.

"Stephen,
with spirit strong
you delighted your family
with laughter
and song.

"Stephen,
on Mother's Day
I felt your strong spirit
pass away,
pass by.

"Stephen,
our beautiful son,
Lord, help us to know
how to live
alone."

After one leaves our lives, we speak of emptiness, of being lonely, sometimes even when with people. Perhaps I knew loneliness but, as Mel wrote, *aloneness* was dominant, a change that I felt in my relation to others. I was different, I thought, because my son was dead.

Friendships changed. A few were lost, most were constant, two or three largely were responsible for my recovery. "What is a friend? It is a person with whom you dare to be yourself. Your soul can be naked with him . . . You can sin with him, laugh with him, pray with him. Best of all you can keep still with him." (C. Raymond Beran)

"Your whole being just screams for help and there's so little anyone can do except to be there, be someone to lean on, to be a good listener," wrote one.

Screams. Once a friend related her cure for frustration. "I walk out to the backyard, open my mouth wide and just scream silently until all the hurt comes out."

"And does it?" I asked.

"You bet!"

Recurrently I uttered silent screams until my eyeballs bulged and my head throbbed. As with many prescriptions, the act did alleviate symptoms; better, neighbors' sensitivities were not ruffled by my inaudible ravings.

There was irony in our discovery of a check stub and its attendant letter, mailed to Paula's grandmother following the death of her husband, and later shared with us.

25 March 19—
Dear Mrs. A—,
I'm sorry this is late but I have been incarcerated in the hospital for over two weeks, now feeling well and anxious to leave, but the doctors are just as determined to keep me here. I should like to express my sorrow at your loss and hope this small gift will help to lessen yours. Perhaps my contribution to this worthy organization may someday help prevent someone else's loss.
My sincerest regards,
Stephen C. Lantz, Midshipman 2/c USN

Seven weeks afterward, our county unit of the American Cancer Society would begin to tally dollars in his memory.

Nestled among one day's sympathy cards was a billing from the hospital at Andrews Air Force Base which requested Now Delinquent payment for room and board. Grimly pondering its disposal, we relegated it to the CACO, the Casualty Affairs Calls Officer of the U.S. Navy.

On our return from Arlington the officer had telephoned for an appointment to schedule shipment of Steve's belongings, close his bank accounts and to arrange disbursements of insurance and Social Security funds. Although I realized the necessity of our meeting, I had no desire to become acquainted with survivor's benefits. I knew no benefit in surviving, nor did I want any monies. After his visits I appreciated the difficulty of this officer's job, his empathy and skillful handling of long-distance details. A similarly trained individual might be helpful to civilians. *To take over* means to relieve, and that was his role. However, compensation, pre-stipulated by Stephen to be mailed in installments, would remind us thirty-six times of the reason for its coming and evoke feelings not unlike those prompted by the shipment from the Naval Academy.

Duly inventoried and carefully packed in two gigantic cardboard boxes, the personal effects of one Midshipman 2nd Class came home. Meticulously hung, rolled and stowed in one small closet and a desk at Bancroft Hall, the accumulation ranged from full uniforms to scraps of paper with penciled jottings. I read every word of those final, hand written contacts.

Stephen's college/service life paraded in slow-motion review as we unpacked. I had wondered what a mother or spouse of a military deceased experienced receiving boxes like these. The feeling is nearly indescribable, like exposing an unfamiliar facet of that person, almost like invading his or her privacy. And what to do with a superabundance of regulation clothing, books, souvenirs?

Upset and overwhelmed by utter volume, I desperately wanted to disperse some contents quickly. We retained a few military items; but with the CACO's assistance, the remainder was sorted for return to the Academy or to the used clothing distribution center of another Naval base. A few articles were set aside for those who might want a tangible memory. Yet to be tackled was Steve's bedroom, but that could wait until tomorrow or tomorrow, or tomorrow.

> One day in the ICU I said, "Son, You and I have never been very long on patience. Maybe this time we will need to be." Lord, give me patience and bring me peace as You brought it to Stephen, while I wait, while I wait.
>
> The summer skies have never been bluer with brilliant slashes of vermilion at sunset tonight. The evening air sneaks through the open door bringing perfumed memories of the day's flowers. The golden glow of street lights bathes the slumbering neighborhood in softness and peace. I see the beauty but my heart beats with great thunder rolls which threaten to smother me. When the storm [of grief] is over, will there be

a rainbow?

Do not cry so loudly, my soul, and you will hear comfort. Quiet whispers of consolation come with the evening. In the solitude I hear best and know rest.

> Day
> awakens the mind
> which seeks new
> meanings,
> grills it in light.
>
> Night
> cradles the soul
> which cries out
> for peace,
> wraps it in stars.

Steve's memento-crammed bedroom opposite ours was silent because he had spent only brief vacations at home for the past three years. Nevertheless, I did not now plan to sterilize it or the rest of the house of his photographs, school art, books, models or snapshots. These tangibles eventually would replace tears from remembering with smiles. And his bedroom would always be called *Steve's room.*

"I know if I were you, I would not spend my days in this house. I don't know how you'll stand it. Maybe you'll want to do something different this summer," Mel had suggested soon after Stephen's death. I usually anticipated the season when volunteer and social activities subsided; however, this year a less crowded schedule did not excite me. I needed a plan to inject empty hours with tasks, not torment.

The usual complement of outdated, dog-eared magazines had spilled over end tables in the ICU waiting room at Bethesda. A reprint in one concerned *Make Today Count,* the national organization founded by Orville Kelly who concentrated on living although dying from incurable lymphocytic lymphoma. His positivity was contagious and I intended to discuss with Stephen his participation in a local chapter, once he attained remission. Even when it became obvious that he would not join a group, the philosophies lingered; and during our final day at the Medical Center, I filched the magazine.[4]

- *Talk about it. Call it death. You can't make life normal again by avoiding the word.*
- *Accept death as a part of life. It is.*
- *Wholly accept one gift of each day: study a butterfly, hear complete silence, absorb a thought, be drenched in a lush melody, aroma or flavor, watch a toddler playing alone.*
- *Accept the unalterable fact that life isn't perfect.*
- *Pray if you wish. Cry if you must. Weakness is not born of either.*
- *Learn to live with yourself, your strengths and weaknesses.*
- *Put your relatives and friends at ease for they are coping too.*
- *Continue to plan for the future. Although you are convinced yours has ended, it hasn't.*
- *Do one constructive task each day.*
- *Discuss your feelings with someone who will listen; also listen to another.*

And I added: Look outside your pain, into another's need. And levy a bit of levity, a dash of humor, against a somber mood.

My *Make Today Count* offensive was launched on household and garden chores neglected for two months. The profusion of spring plants choking the flower beds surely proved the persistence of life; but I derived perverse pleasure in killing, yanking weeds away from their more attractive neighbors, thereby finding a safe method to vent hostility. Plants given as living memorials nurtured me as I tended them: the rose bush, appropriately named "American Heritage," an ever green dwarf spruce, a weeping fig tree and a weeping larch bonsai.

How befitting their names, their selections for us, but who first dubbed beautiful, cascading plants with permanent grief? Perennials wanted dividing and herbs from my kitchen garden awaited cultivation and drying. Years earlier, a neighbor had teased about my season-long toil in the soil. "Doing a lot of praying again this year, I see." Close to truth, for hands-and-knees gardening is akin to a religious experience, with even more significance for me this summer.

After routine maintenance, I tackled projects: stripping and rewaxing oak floors, sorting old magazines for riddance or reference, de-cluttering drawers, cupboards and closets of unused articles, arranging a jumble of photos into albums, cataloging a twenty-year conglomeration of travel brochures. Realizing the cathartic benefits of physical activity, I exhorted myself to work; but apathy, that also numbs the grief-stricken, prolonged my jobs throughout the summer.

I filled quiet hours with writing a few acknowledgments each day, listening to records or reading: *Eric,* the story of a leukemic youth; several publications by Dr. Elisabeth Kübler-Ross; *Life After Life; The Bible;* books selected from Steve's library or his original writings, as if their ingestion might somehow bring closeness.

"Why am I keeping all this stuff?" he had wondered as he sorted and stashed compositions.

"Because one day, years from now, you'll enjoy reading how you felt about things at a particular age, or your children or grandchildren will," I had replied. Or your mother will. Once he reviewed the hereafter as described in the Koran.

"In the Islamic view of Heaven it appears to be a very beautiful place, like a paradise on earth '. . . gardens of a dark green . . . fruits and palm trees and pomegranates . . . in attendance are youths who shall continue in their bloom forever.' This seems like a very pleasing home. However, being a non-Muslim I apparently will never see this place. Perhaps it's just as well. I'm kind of partial to white robes, harps and clouds." Youths in their bloom forever *was appealing to me, as I read his paper.*

Mel, Valeri and I were avidly drawn to explanations of what happened to Stephen's life when it left the ICU. We professed Christian belief in life after death; now we sought documentation through secular literature.

". . . elevated and harmonious thoughts dominated and united the individual images . . . and a divine calm swept through my soul . . . Everything was transfigured as though by a heavenly light and everything was beautiful, without grief, without anxiety and without pain. . . ."
ALBERT VON ST. GALLEN-HEIM, "REMARKS ON FATAL FALLS," 1892.

Prior to her demise, a teen-age leukemic patient in a local hospital composed her concept of meeting with Death.

". . . sirens calling me with their
sweet, enchanting song
Then suddenly I see a light
It beckons me to come.
I no longer stand on ground.

I no longer see the ocean.
I am lifted by the light
And guided to its source.
While my body lies in a coma
My mind is free to roam
Into the ultimate beauty.
I step over the threshold
And back in the hospital
I die."

Several persons, resuscitated after being pronounced dead, have recounted their postmortem impressions. Although admitting that the other-dimensional state was nearly impossible to describe explicitly, many agreed about elements of the posthumous environment. When one dies he may see himself disembodied, floating above the death-site or in an impenetrably dark void and realizing awesome isolation from severed communication with the living. Unpleasant auditory sensations such as piercing whistles, buzzing or ringing may temporarily jar him. As he undergoes incredibly rapid transit through a black hole or tunnel, he may be aware of other presences guiding his transition from death to life. He meets a Being of Light, one with a special identity who opens his mind fully to self-understanding and universal truth. Vivid imageries of his life are scanned in a fast-forward mode of flashback. Finally, in ultimate tranquility the deceased embraces higher consciousness and crosses the border of no return.[5]

Reading about those who fleetingly looked across that border and returned to describe their experiences added dimension to our perspectives of an existence beyond an earthly life.

A mandate from Steve's local funeral service urged, "Nerve thy heart and trembling soul to do that which will comfort other souls than thine." During our weeks as strangers in Bethesda, a Red Cross volunteer regularly had inquired about and met our needs for functioning in a strange community. Now, in my distress, I was motivated to help someone. Almost in reply, the church newsletter solicited lay visitors for hospitalized members.

"As you know, I have recently spent three weeks at a hospital. I'm not sure I can handle visitation, but I'd like to try," I approached the minister.

"Naturally you would not share your recent problem," was his only admonishment.

The following week I began calls at two hospitals. I listened to symptoms, pains and complaints, but more often heard words of determination to conquer whatever adversity had brought people there. "Complete these dear, unfinished tasks of mine and I, perchance, may therein comfort you."

When friends learned of my new volunteerism, some reacted: "I couldn't do that. Of course, I see my family or friends if they're in the hospital, but there's something about that place. . . ." I wanted to advise they blot out hospital halitosis, hovering odors which recall unpleasant procedures and medical traumas. Concentrate instead on the essence of caring that you bring; and cock a receptive ear, not a critical nose to help erase a few lonely moments for a bedbound visitee.

Valeri trained for Volunteen duty and began weekly pediatric service with older children and youth. I wondered at her fortitude as she described one tableau: a father sitting beside his sleeping, bald and emaciated, leukemic son who had come out of remission—and the empty bed she noted the following week.

One day as I entered the room to revisit an older patient, I was shocked by the sight of an empty bed. The episode repeated, and for a third and fourth time this summer. Although logic said otherwise, I began to feel that my calls were precursors to death's. To lessen my emotional involvement and add variety in service, I completed Red Cross and hospital training courses that prepared me for volunteer hospital and bloodmobile assignments.

Former entertainment like television, movies, theater or social gatherings provided little diversion to Mel and me; but we frequented parks, woods and beaches to immerse ourselves in the serenity and continuity of Nature, tantamount to what we struggled to recapture. "Pain is easier to endure out in the open. Space draws it from you. Enclosure squeezes it close."[6] And planned or spontaneous, a quiet hour with a friend usually parried depression.

Thus, I programmed myself to re-live, and exhausted from the expanded activity level, I needed neither tranquilizers nor sleep inducements!

The firsts. The first birthday, Thanksgiving, Christmas. Although tradition dictates their observances, the perpetuation of any family custom soon after the death of one of its members annuls holiday jollity. Never before so acutely perceived, we had already endured Memorial Day, with its ritual honoring of the military deceased, and Father's Day with emotions of its own.

Thinking that our outing to the local fairgrounds on the evening of July 4 would not produce the emotional impact of the other *firsts,* we spread a blanket under a fusillade of fire showers and bursting bombs. I underestimated the salvos from grief. Even the smallest opportunity will unleash them. Near the splendid, patriotic finale, gloom came to sit by me; but my recall of the Bicentennial nudged it aside.

> *By 10:00 a.m. we were four among the affable throng of a million and a half who had gathered in Washington, D.C. We would feel stimulation from the scene and relief after hour-*

long waits for food and bathroom privileges. Lacking jackets to ward off the unforeseen, unseasonable chill that swept across the capital Mall during the fireworks, we huddled against the exterior wall of the National Archives building. A four-hour wait for public transportation to our car in the commuter lot was capping the sixteen-hour day. "Where in heck are the buses?" Mel quizzed a harried policeman. Spying a label that protruded from our bedraggled, brown lunch bag, he only answered, "Can I have a cookie?" We retired at 5:00 a.m. July 5, but exhaustion yielded to exhilaration for having been part of that celebration and because of Stephen's induction into the Navy at Annapolis on 6 July!

Parents, sisters, brothers and friends witnessed thirteen hundred ill-composed, white uniformed neophytes who intoned the Oath of Office at the late afternoon ceremony. As the strains of the "Navy Blue and Gold" concluded the formalities and we concluded our visit, Stephen looked alone, vulnerable, even frightened—expressions heretofore foreign to him. This second sixteen-hour day had been only a grueling preamble to a normal Plebe summer.

Phone conversations and letters were infrequent, but when we heard, the news was upbeat.

"For the first time in five days I am able to relax. Today has been Heaven (being Sunday helped). This past week has been a nightmare. I didn't think I would be able to stand it, but with help I know I can hack it. I am determined to stick it out until the end, and I will not fail! Dad, you were right. It took about three weeks to get comfortable with this [military] system. . . .

      (I love writing that)
      Stephen C. Lantz, Midshipman, USN"

Months later I asked if he had been homesick. "Not really, except that first night. I stretched out on my rack [bed] with my arms crossed behind my head and stared into the dark. You all had left, and I said to myself, What the Hell am I doing here?

After that I never had time to be homesick. Sure I missed everyone—the family, my friends, home, all those good times we had. But there's compensation with my new friends and challenges, and with the fact that I'm where I want to be, learning what I want to do most—be a Naval officer, and I'm lucky!" Like climactic pyrotechnics on the Fourth of July, Stephen's high school dreams and goals had exploded into a brilliant finale.

> When Steve left home [for college] I did not cry. I had time to prepare for his going and was proud he was able to do what he most wanted—his talents to be offered, his goals realized, so right for him. Now I cry often. Out of self pity? Out of what we and the world have lost? Sorrow because he didn't want to die? Does anyone? We who are left don't seek death but may live a moment apart from it until the moment together.
> At the lake today I watched the clouds softly jostling and the waves gently tumbling—always changing, ever renewing, never dying. I thought of the fragility of man. We believe we have eternal life. Do we know God throughout eternity, before and after this life? Why do we even come here? And as we strolled the shore, Mel conjectured. "I've asked myself the same questions. One possible answer that keeps recurring is that perhaps there are some experiences and lessons we can know only here." I agree. And then we have to leave?

Unanswered questions, from generation to generation. Stephen's doubts also had surfaced in a creative writing assignment.

> "Sometimes I lie awake and wonder about life. For what purpose have I been placed in this world? This once beautiful planet is now spoiled by man's carelessness and indifference. The foul air, the stinking water, the devastated land. Is it possible to salvage anything out of the chaos that five thousand years of civilization have made? What can I do for my fellow man and more important, do I want to do anything? Do I give a damn what happens to mankind after I'm gone? Does anyone give a damn?
> "Sometimes I wonder about all the hard work. What's it for anyway? One just dies in the end. Is there really a God and does He reward hard workers and punish lazy, good-for-nothing

bastards, or are we all going to the same place and just don't know it? I get depressed when I think about this, but I take courage from the knowledge that personal achievement is a blessing and waste a curse."

The excuse for a family gathering on my birthday held greater appeal than adding years to my total; but this summer I strongly hoped the date would be ignored. The past pained. Hanging in the hall were three Norman Rockwell prints of a wedding, a birthday party and a picnic, a gift that Steve selected as reminders of our family's happiest occasions. Recordings, books and handcrafts created by his fingers should have been apprized, not now viewed with regret for no more to come. Our last family dinner on my birthday had begun at sunset in the revolving restaurant atop the lofty Canadian National Tower in Toronto, and had ended long after the winking points of starlight above and men's lights below escorted dusk to dark.

Never again.

But no one ignored my day. *Au contraire,* more than ever they showered me with new keepsakes to cache; and my seventy-nine year old, visually-impaired father recited his poem which lifted my depression because it emphasized the importance of each to another.

> "Most days are born to live and die,
> Then, shrouded by night's velvet sky,
> Join all the ghosts of other days,
> Wand'ring, lost in mem'ry's maze.
> Then came a day and there was you,
> A living soul, so soft and new,
> That caused us to set each day apart,
> Cherished deep within our hearts.
> Since then each day shall ever be
> To us a living memory."

"The God that made it possible for you to create and to love your son can in some time and in some way comfort," a friend had written. To create. But when Stephen died, sexual desire died also. I had heard that parents are encouraged to enlarge their family when a child dies. Years earlier Mel and I had limited ours, but I could not now envision ever creating another child who also might die. Still, I needed to separate confused emotions and motivations as I painstakingly worked toward rekindling sexual expression as a demonstration of love.

Stephen was conceived in our love for each other, our happiness with each other. Sometimes it seems that love has been shrinking as it has been expanding to three, then four. Was it too shallow to allow expansion? is it too shallow to survive?

When love dies, we die. Now we don't seem to care enough to make love. Is it too soon? Why are we content to let this happen, to die while still alive? Does death limit love? Love is supposed to grow. How long ago did ours begin to be stunted?

"There is nothing in all creation that will ever be able to separate us from the love of God," was a quotation from the memorial service. Nothing can separate us from each other as finally as death. There may be nothing more difficult to handle.

Death erases our problems, brings peace to our souls, allows us to rejoice in new life—all benefits for the deceased! The survivor's mind rails against the injustice of death. At the hospital today I overheard someone discussing an affront. "If you're looking for justice, you're living in the wrong world." There is no human justice in Stephen's illness and death. But perhaps we are wrong to pursue it. Like the painter. Reproached by a woman who accused him of not doing her justice in the realistic portrait just unveiled, he retorted: "Madam, I have done you justice. What you really seek is mercy." Perhaps we should seek God's mercy.

Death is the murderer of communication. It makes the asset of memory the best comfort, and "memories should not be kept in drawers," was a line of dialogue in the movie we saw tonight. So, I must not only continue to remember, but keep retrieving funny and fun-filled memories, even when Do you remember when? is sad and glad, all at once.

Nine years ago, on a sultry April day in the Ozarks: The rock-strewn, boulder-pitted dirt road to the top of petite Baird Mountain was too strenuous for our Chevy's round legs, one already having succumbed from the gash of a sharp, flint chip. So we parked and hiked the final mile and a half to the ridge where we passed the day basking our chilled, northern bodies, collecting fossilized rocks, relishing our picnic and saving moments on film. With stones, Steve spelled his name and that of a current girlfriend for the gliding hawks to read.

Anticipating a quick dip in the still frigid lake at our motel, we reluctantly left this idyllic setting. To our dismay we realized that only another mile and a half trek to the summit would recoup the motel key and another forgotten item! Finally en route to our room, we harmonized our new words to a familiar folk tune.

> On top of Baird Mountain
> All covered with rocks,
> I left my motel key
> and a pair o' dirty socks.
> The socks were so smelly!
> I left them in fun.
> I shouldn't 'a done it
> 'cause that's poll-u-tion.

What delight we knew in Stephen's life; what delight we know in Valeri's. Will You take her back, too soon? "Sometimes the good die young and that we can do nothing about."

I yearn for the peace God brought Stephen. I would die to achieve it, but that is not my fate, yet. I believed in Fate [like the Plan of the Creator] . When we have served our purpose, nothing can save us from our destiny. Part of Stephen's destiny was to be buried in his D and B uniform with full military honors, gold anchors and stars.^D *I am not comfortable with Fate's call now; the belief brings a heavy burden.*

Long ago I ceased worrying about making the right decisions to realize my purposes in life. With my plans and the Lord's help, my goals were met: education, jobs, marriage, children. The decisions were right; I didn't look back. Then some of those purposes began dissolving in tears because of the loss of one surrogate, purpose-filler. Now I realize that Stephen fulfilled his purpose, but his was not mine. I guess I wanted his to be mine. His must count as a part of mine, but mine goes further. Where? Since I am still alive, is it because my assignment is incomplete?

Someone visiting Steve in his hospital room commented, "This may be a real test for you." "No," he replied, "this will be a real test for the doctors!" Is his death God's test for me? I sometimes feel like Steve before he got his sea legs when he wrote during that youngster cruise, "I had trouble ashore last night. The whole damned island kept rolling and pitching."

Thank you, Lord, for allowing Stephen to be a part of our lives for awhile. Help us to learn to love his memory without such grief. Help us to regain our lost dreams without his encouragement. Help us to love You as we loved him. That I do not do.

A niece who stood beside us at Arlington must ve known that if I could not travel the miles to Stephen's grave, my thoughts went there often that summer. As I read the letter and enclosed poem she sent before her return to college, I wondered if the sentiments would set the tenor of the approaching season.

> Do not stand at my grave and weep—
> I am not there, I do not sleep.
> I am a thousand winds that blow;
> I am the diamond glints on snow.
> I am sunlight on ripened grain,
> I am the gentle autumn's rain.
> When you waken in the morning's blush,
> I am the swift, uplifting rush
> Of quiet birds in circled flight,
> I am the soft star that shines at night.
> Do not stand at my grave and cry—
> I am not there, I did not die.   AUTHOR UNKNOWN

Like the binding on my journal, tasks and thoughts spiraled through summer hours. Work and play held anguish at bay, but it always circled back. The days gradually shortened; my notations evidenced neither abridgment nor alleviation of pain.

> The calendar tells me fall is nearing tho' the weather doesn't, yet. I hope there aren't many rainy days this fall. Rain is tears.
> Stephen died in the spring. Now my favorite azaleas will always remind me of him, two blazing plants inside his room and hundreds more outside to surround illness and dying with beauty.
> As we walked that long, central hall after midnight 13 May, I knew the true meaning of deathly quiet. Yet, the contrast outdoors triggered another feeling: It was a time of rebirth, not death.
> These thoughts I kept repeating. They do not change my sorrow for long. I still feel like fall.

Memorial

*I take a special moment
out of every lonely day.
And I think about a friend I had
taken suddenly away.
We had my friend so short a time
He went so fast, it seems a crime.
This song is for Steve,
My friend I do believe,
And I'll weep now, if I may . . .*

*And I don't know why, Lord;
It's like you never tried, Lord;
It makes me want to cry, Lord;
Why did he have to die?*

*I walked with an old man
beneath a summer sky.
His face rough when I kissed him
and a twinkle in his eye.
This grumpy old man went so fast
His voice still echoes in my past.
This is for Grandpa John,
He has died, but is not gone.
But sometimes, I still cry . . .*

*I did not even see what was
the most painful loss.
A man was scourged and terrified
and hanging on a cross.
Yet with His last breath
He triumphed over death.
May His life reach us.
This song is for Jesus.
Comfort us today.*

*And I really know why, Lord;
I know how hard You've tried, Lord;
But sometimes I still cry, Lord;
Why did he have to die?
Help me.
Keep my faith alive.*

COPYRIGHT © 1979 by JOHN AND STEVEN MACDONALD

Autumn

". . . their souls dwell in the house of tomorrow which you cannot visit, not even in your dreams." GIBRAN

Nature has not been so lovely for a long time, or did I notice it more this year? Last spring the Maryland azaleas were jewels among the grey folds of our sorrow and the prickly pear at home blazed [in July] with dozens of newborn sons and daughters, all yellow gold. The delicate hues of Steve's rose were an overture to the robust ruby tones of their old neighbors. Mourning doves plaintively repeated their morning hymns and evensongs, more constantly than I can remember. In memoriam. Peridots, emeralds and jade clustered on stickpin branches to pierce the sapphire heights, arch overhead while we hiked.

Near home, familiar faces and places soothed during a summer paced without the trauma of Bethesda. Normally off-season vacationers, we preferred less crowded highways, accommodations and interest areas. Now, since vacations like holidays also would evoke the past, I had little inclination to travel. Still, as accelerated fall schedules loomed, I felt we should escape from the everyday. We invited Paula and a friend of Valeri's to share a late August week among northern woods and waters where beachcombing, canoeing, fishing and unregimented hours might further wholeness. But distress stowed away in my travel gear.

In town this afternoon my attention riveted on the vulgar outburst of an ill-kempt young man. Silently I censured him, Why are you alive? But in the next moment I chastised my own vulgarity. When I see toddlers on the beach, I see Stephen at that age. My heart aches as I remember first sand castles, then forts. When I look in their eyes I see innocence, and can smile. We need to feel like children again. We lose our youth too soon and spend the rest of our lives searching for it. "It takes a very long time to be young." (Pablo Picasso)

Summer is over. Tomorrow Valeri begins high school. Steve began that chapter six years ago. This was his first entire summer away. Have a good year dear Stephen, wherever you are.
"Strange is it not? that of the myriads who
Before us pass'd the door of Darkness through,
Not one returns to tell us of the Road,
Which to discover we must travel too."
RUBAIYAT OF OMAR KHAYYAM

The September issue of The Shipmate *(USNA alumni magazine) arrived today. "See 'Last Call.'" The attached card referred me to the obituaries: "They shall not grow old as we that are left grow old; age shall not worry them nor the years condemn; at the going down of the sun and in the morning we will remember them. . . ." (from the Scottish Tomb of the Unknown Soldier, Edinburgh) True. Every night and the first thought of morning is Stephen is dead. Another midshipman is listed in the columns, too. I wonder how he died.*
How sobering to be pallbearer for a best friend and peer,

especially when one is near twenty-one. Eight young men and women who attended Steve at home and ten more at the Academy must have felt more than grief and loss.

Later a call from Paula. "I have sad news. Yesterday Pat N— was killed in a plane accident in California." Dear God. Sometimes the good die young.

Only four months before, Patrick had spoken at the Annapolis memorial service. We had known him as one of Steve's friends in the Drum and Bugle Corps and as one who visited at Bethesda. Just a month earlier we had received a sympathy letter from his mother, whom I had never met.

"We remember hearing about Steve and had met him. We were happy that he was also an Exchange Youth.ᴱ Pat was pleased to do the Reflections, rather, I should say, honored...."

I know an urgency to attend Pat's services at Annapolis and Arlington. Valeri must feel it, too, for she asked to miss school and go with me. Some doubts. Why do I go? The replay will be sad, but I sense we will find comfort once again in those places. I reread Mrs. N's letter.

"We cannot feel exactly as others do at certain traumatic periods in our lives, but my husband and I have been deeply moved by Steve's passing. There but for the Grace of God...."

Now there is no doubt about our return, but tonight I do not cry for Stephen or Patrick. They are shipmates once again.

> One ship drives east and another west
> with selfsame winds that blow;
> It's the set of the sail and not the gale
> that tell them where to go.
> Like the winds of the sea and the winds of fate,
> as we voyage along through life,
> It's the set of the sail that decides its goal,
> And not the calm or the strife. AUTHOR UNKNOWN

Three days later our plane to Washington, D.C. streaked into a bright azure canopy above a checkerboard of greens and browns, fall-tinged woodlots and shimmering, silver water splotches, all linked with dark lacings and white ribbons that alluded to our spring land transits.

Dashing from an Academy parking lot to the copper-domed chapel, I felt invigorated. Did adrenalin surge from tight travel connections or from the tension of being unable to predict my response to what lay ahead? Many astonished faces that greeted Val and me were the same we had met in May, but Pat's service was held in St. Andrew's Chapel beneath the nave of the main one.

Pensive, some of us lingered afterward in an upstairs aisle. A midshipman ruefully puzzled, "I don't understand what's happening, Mrs. Lantz. Maybe God's going to start his own Drum and Bugle Corps." I recalled a poem which had been sent to us by a friend. In this ancient Rig-Veda, a sacred Hindu writing, a warrior laments the loss of a comrade.

> *From the dead hand I take the bow he wielded*
> *To gain for us dominion, might and glory.*
> *Thou there, we here, rich in heroic offspring,*
> *Will vanquish all assaults of every foeman.*
> *Approach the bosom of the earth, the mother,*
> *This earth extending far and most propitious;*
> *Young, soft as wool to bounteous givers, may she*
> *Preserve thee from the lap of dissolution.*
> *Open wide, O earth, press not heavily upon him,*
> *Be easy of approach, hail him with kindly aid;*
> *As with a robe a mother hides*
> *Her son, so shroud this man, O earth.*

Strolling the shaded, brick walk, we crossed the blossom-decked Yard (campus) to the museum to see the contents of a velvet-backed display. *The first personally owned ring of any class to be donated to the museum becomes the permanent representative of that class in this collection.* The identification on the back of the case, *Midn. Stephen C. Lantz, USN,* triggered visceral spasms. His was the only midshipman's ring in the collection.

That evening we dined with Pat's fiancée and his family, spoke of our sons' birthdates (both in January), their deaths and special incidents in their lives. Strangely, we could laugh, too.

Pondering whether or not to mention it, I was struck with the quandary of the query, *What will you do with Pat's ring?* But its placement arose during normal conversation, and Stephen's band soon had an adjacent neighbor.

The following noon the motorcade retraced the forty-miles from Annapolis to Arlington, but my concentration was more on driving in traffic than trafficking in remorse. Coincidentally, we approached the cemetery intersection of Porter and MacArthur Avenues. Val and I were surprised to see that Stephen and Patrick would lie in diagonal plots across one road. "Close enough for signal flags," I wryly observed. Phrases re-consoled, horns re-echoed.

Scarcely more than a year before Steve had written, "They just played 'Tattoo' outside my window which comes five minutes before 'Taps'. I do love bugle calls. Oh, 'Taps' just started. What a beautiful melody. I think I'll have them play it at my funeral, whenever that is."

Near the conclusion of this graveside ceremony, I was awash with discordant emotions. Whenever casket flags were bestowed on wives or mothers in films and newsreels, I had been an observer. Earlier this year I had been a stunned recipient, stunned partly because we who are military next of kin prefer to ignore the possibility of our becoming a receiver of that flag. Yet I, too, had clutched it to my breast with esteem for its significance and for that of the colors of the Drum and Bugle Corps, the flag Steve had carried, also presented to me. As I witnessed Mrs. N— this day, I envisioned American burial flags as lanyards that bind together all who have given a part of themselves in service to their country.

Afterward, as some of us walked to Stephen's grave, I unconsciously vocalized my journal notation. "Well, Pat and Steve are shipmates again."

"We all still are, ma'am," was a young lieutenant-instructor's quiet reply.

In rows of thousands, the renowned and the ordinary are gathered from dissimilar episodes of similar service, their legions termlessly at parade rest in the real military archives of a nation. For the first time Valeri and I read the words chiseled on one among identical white granite slabs, and we sobbed in each other's arms. The night of our return home I wrote,

Dear Steve,

I wish you didn't die.

Val and I have returned from Pat's services. The weather was warm and sunny. The flight was perfect. The Yard brimmed with color. Your ring in the museum was beautiful; your friends, now ours, so caring. Chaplain B's words, Arlington and 'Taps,' all beautiful. We had tough moments but agreed our visit made us feel good, too. We felt you there. Now we are back. The weather is still beautiful. Dad and home are, too. My throat tightens and hot tears flow again.

I wish you didn't die.

Mortals are like books in the lending library of God's world. But all creation, creatures, plants are loaned, not given to us. Life is loaned like a fine painting or a rare book. It is not to be disposed of as we wish, to be toyed with, used and thrown away. It is to be appreciated, loaned to others, but always returned to the library. No doubt there will be fines if the loan isn't returned in good condition because of the borrower's abuse. It may be returned early, on time, or over-due, but it must be returned. God is always searching for lost books, always printing new ones, always reviewing the collection.

A neighbor, whose son had been killed by a hit-and-run driver some years earlier, sympathized with Mel one afternoon as each paused in his lawn mowing. During their conversation Mel probed, "Was your grief different somehow because you have other sons, while I had but one?"

"I could not say, of course; but I doubt it because each is special and can never be replaced."

I know my convictions about eternal life are stronger than ever, now that Stephen has left our world. We intend to see him again. Might we be a family? We hope we have the patience and direction to lead us to the beauty of that reunion. My dad says, "To me, Steve is just on a longer cruise. I piped him aboard the first time he came home on leave; and one day he's going to walk in that front door again, throw his arms *around me with a big hug like he always did and say, 'Hi, Paw-Paw.'"* Oh, what a day that would be for us all!

"Never let yesterday use up today,
Live for the moment,
Learn to grow and change in the present
And to let the past go gently." AUTHOR UNKNOWN

"For yesterday is but a dream
And tomorrow is only a vision.
But today, well lived, Makes every day
a dream of happiness And every tomorrow
a vision of hope." SANSKRIT PROVERB

Today I wrote again to Steve's friends. Like returning to the Academy, writing to them makes me feel closer to him. Each day I watch for the mail as avidly as when we hoped to hear from him; selfishly, I hope they need us, too. Everyone knows what a good correspondent Steve was. Maybe we follow his example. Many of his Navy friends have new assignments. I used to think how Steve would miss them this ac (academic) year. Irony.

"Not a day goes by that I don't think of Steve and you all. Every time I get in my boat I think of him because the last thing he said to me at Bethesda was, I'll be there; and I know he is with me. I know that I can't take his place—no one can—but I would like to keep in touch and make you a part of my life."

"I am sure that you have heard many say how some good was gained despite the tragedy, and I'm no exception. Because of my visit to Bethesda, I learned to evaluate things in a new light. I learned that a Darth Vader costume can be used to brighten the lives of others. Since Bethesda, I have been to two hospitals and a handicapped children's camp. I have tried to put myself in your position. . . it made me more appreciative of the family ties that I have. I hope I will continue to hear from you. It's strange, but for the short time I knew you, it really means a lot."

The thirteenth of the month is drawing near again. The Mids would say BOHICA [Bend Over, Here It Comes Again]. And again I sit weeping. Like flying to Pat's services—plunging into opaque towers of cloud-fluff and breaking out suddenly into brightness—I have passed the months between clouds of memory and the harshness of reality.

Today I wrote the last four letters about his death to old friends and received one in reply. "You seem to be adjusting well to your grief, but I am angry and deeply hurt." We are deeply hurt, and angry, too, I suppose. But my tears come more from hurt. At least these are the ones I acknowledge. I have no happiness alone nor with groups, though I know some with the family or a single friend. It is inconceivable to consider hosting a party or enjoying someone else's. I struggle to find lasting pleasure anywhere. I cannot say I ever have been happy these months, but it's easier now to find peace.

At age forty I tackled my lifelong goal to study piano. Few are motivated to longer practice sessions than mine for those five years.

Valeri and I painstakingly rehearsed a rousing duet of "Anchors Aweigh" for Stephen's [first Christmas] homecoming. Last year, as I showed off a bit of Shubert to Paula and him, he applauded, "You're doing great, Mom, better every time I come home." The knife wrenches. Never again will I hear his comments. And my body pulses only the rhythms of dirges. I cannot play the piano. I have no desire to be creative. I am less grief-filled when doing mundane chores. It's not enough. To laugh again, wholeheartedly; to love again, deeply; to remember again without tears; to live fully—What may salve?

I appreciate some things more: Val's struggles to mature; Mel's vibes, feelings that leak out but are, as yet, rarely verbalized; the grandeur of a cloud bank; understanding in a friend's eyes. "In search of serenity." Steve's appointment calendar had that picture caption opposite 13 May.

Death levels one accustomed to being in control, one filled with ego strength, one with an opinion about almost everything. I reread phrases [from a Jewish Day of Atonement service] and continue my search for serenity.

"Shall I cry out in anger, O God,
Because Thy gifts are mine but for awhile?

. . . When a fate beyond my understanding takes from me
Friends and kin whom I have cherished, and leaves me
Bereft of shining presences that have lit my way
Through years of companionship and affection. . . .

Those I have loved, though now beyond my view,
Have given form and quality to my being,
And they live on, unfailingly feeding
My heart, and mind, and imagination.

They have led me into the wide Universe
I continue to inhabit,
And their presence is more vital to me
than their absence.

What Thou givest O Lord, Thou takest not away,
And bounties once granted shed their radiance
evermore. . . ."

The previous fall Steve had written, "The summer was so busy, I really wasn't ready for school to start. But, here it is and I kinda got caught with my pants down! I'm *behind* in everything! Never fear. I can handle anything I set my mind to, I think." I, too, saw discrepancy between the progress I thought I should be making and how I felt.

Five months. It seems five years. The clock chimes twelve, the dawn of his final battle. I relive that day a hundred times. I didn't want Steve to suffer more and I do not want him back as he was. We were not afraid for him, nor did he seem afraid. I know death would seem sweet to me, were I he, once reconciled to leaving. But death is never sweet to us who stay behind. Maybe his leaving will sweeten our departure when it comes, if we can hold him again. Were it not for Valeri, it could not come too soon. Somehow I must believe I'm needed here and live.

> "Whatever crazy sorrow saith,
> No life that breathes with human breath
> Has ever truly longed for death.
>
> "'Tis life, whereof our nerves are scant,
> Oh life, not death, for which we pant;
> More life, and fuller, that I want."   ALFRED TENNYSON

Death is like a revolution against life. At its climax we must find freedom. A freedom Stephen sorely lacked was from bad cells. What an unfair battle!

For over forty years our church women have sponsored used merchandise sales, the proceeds aiding the needy in local and world communities. This year our family contribution included Stephen's civilian clothing.

> *Sorting clothes at the church tonight, I found Steve's brown corduroy jacket. He didn't wear it much at home; he preferred his old blue ski jackets. "They're comfy and suit me best." We see Stephen in unexpected places, but we mourn because we cannot see him. Does he miss us, too?*
>
> *The night he died I told Valeri, "We will never forget Stephen. He will always be with us, and we will always be the Lantz family." Now he is more constantly in our thoughts than he ever was when he was away at school. How can that be? How can we love him more than before? We are sad because we and the world cannot be touched by him again. Or can it?*
>
> *Reach out and touch someone. I try, but sometimes I feel I'm not touching the ones I love the most, as often as I should. But if Steve had not died, I would not so desperately be reaching out.*

To be greeted indifferently quashes morale; but as a hospital discharge volunteer, I was hailed with *Hurrays* on arriving with a wheelchair to transport patients to the exit. However, some moments would temper my own elevated spirit; an adoring parent with her new son, Stephen; pacing families or people-statues with strained faces, waterstained cheeks; frustrated medics or their despairing charges who were too sick to leave, too despondent to care.

Chaplain D— bolstered me in the elevator today as each went to the next call. "Terminal doesn't only mean end, you know. It also means a place of change, where new directions are taken."

I have not written for awhile. Has time, six months gone, anointed and soothed my wounds? I'm more involved with life now and do not always write before bed, but many nights I think my letters before falling asleep. I promise to record them tomorrow, but morning erases night's slate of memories.

Sometimes Mel and I still cry, but it seems wrong to continue. Yet, we would give anything to return—to touch his hand or stroke his face, to talk quietly, to blow a kiss or feel a swift embrace. We can blow a kiss, but only to a picture, to a memory or the air. We talk positively with others about Steve, but in our aloneness yearn for yesterday. [We would] let some of our yesterdays go gently, but some are wrested from us.

I have greater compassion, but do not feel passion for living. I enjoy its privilege, but still search, not frantically, I hope. A long journey to recovery, I fear. Does L— weep so for Pat? I even pray for strength to cry, so sorrow does not drain me of health nor life.

"I don't really sleep; I think I must die a little each night!" I often joke. If it is my pattern to dream, I am unaware, unlike Valeri and Mel whose night reveries simulate novels. Death effects dreams and nightmares for some; but I was so spent from activity and mourning when bedtime came, my subconscious must have been bankrupted! Thankfully. But one morning a dream summoned vivid recall.

I dreamed a different scenario of Steve's illness and death, and it was strangely real. This time we knew of his cancer, but he continued his work at the Academy. He may have been undergoing treatment or in remission. While the disease had not progressed to the extent it was at Bethesda, he was terminal. His friends knew only that he was ill, not dying.

We came to visit. He said he was very sick sometimes; but he wanted to remain there, not come home. He was happier there. I held him close. We all cried, yet comforted each other. All seemed right. We touched again. I awakened with no heaviness of heart, nor torment of thought. Did he enter my sleeping mind to assuage? I feel so.

Touchdowns and trips, turkeys and Tums, Thanksgiving. After marching in Macy's Christmas parade, the Drum and Bugle Corps once returned to the Academy too late for the holiday feast. The following year Steve quipped, "I'm spending the weekend at D's. No pizza for Thanksgiving this year!" We all remembered trips to Iowa for traditional dinners with grandparents and cousins, and one Thanksgiving weekend in Chicago.

With milling throngs we strolled The Loop and pressed against shop windows dressed to allure, our steam-puff breaths making frosted "O's" under nose prints high and lower on cold glass. Late that evening we bought tickets to the end of the line of nowhere-in-particular and back, so Valeri and Stephen could have their first ride on the El. Next day we sampled ethnic food, music and festivities at the Museum of Science and Industry, and stood enthralled by thirty spiring trees, each trimmed with baubles from a different land. The mischievous finger that pushed all fifteen elevator buttons from our floor to the motel lobby delayed our departure a bit. If I had thought the prank would extend our fun, the finger could have been mine.

Another disquieting *First*. Since Mel had been unable to attend Pat's funeral in September, we planned a late autumn return to the D.C. area. Like Valeri and me, Mel figuratively could remount the horse—confront those places that had so unsettled us, loose feelings, cleanse the hurt and balance perspectives in familiar, but away-from-home space. Contacts with Paula's and Bart's families and other friends would soothe reopened wounds.

Next week we go East. Val remarked it was hard to tell friends just where we were going for Thanksgiving, so East seemed simplest. One does not say she's going to the cemetery for Thanksgiving, yet that is one reason for the trip. We'll visit friends and places with better memories, too, and places of history. Steve became history too soon. Was he part of more than our past? I could believe that.

Not aware of the demise of any governmental official, we asked a Plebe in the Yard why the flag was flying at half-staff the day we revisited the Academy. Airily he replied, "Gee, I dunno. I guess someone died. That seems to happen a lot around here."

At Thanksgiving dinner with Paula's family, we gave thanks for His giving; but I felt some indigestion from having given too much. I do not recall whether or not there were *No, thank you's* among the dishes passed. "No, thank you, I don't care for that, but I will take one spoonful" were acceptable food portions at our home table. As a teen, Stephen had asked, "Mom, how long do I have to have *No, thank you's*?"

I teased, "Until you're a man. No, you're a man now. Probably until you're 21."

Many are the thoughts that come to me
    In my lonely musings;
And they drift so strange and swift,
    There is no time for choosing
    Which to follow . . .
When they come, they come in flocks. . . .
                          RALPH WALDO EMERSON

Winter

> "Be not like others, sore undone, who keep
> long vigil by the silent dust and weep."
> AUTHOR UNKNOWN

The malls were alive with the sounds and sights that formerly heralded my favorite season, but I held at bay the fanfares and festive mood of Christmas. I did not want to think seriously about it. When a potpourri of writings about its meaning was solicited through the church newsletter, though, I dropped my guard. The printing deadline for the booklets passed before my generic reflections were readied, but I had unleashed private torment that continued to erupt as the weeks telescoped toward the Coming. For me, Advent was the worst of *the firsts.*

"Christmas is. . . ."
Christmas is a paradox.

In northern climes Christmas is snow—fluffy mounds of marshmallow cream by day and glistening piles of minute diamonds by night—but only enjoyed by those who have enough clothing to be warm. Snow is a mantle for the Christ-child, a blanket covering a sleeping world which can awaken to new Life come Christmas morn.

Christmas is fragrant greens, some plain and some bejeweled with berry-beads. And Christmas is other good smells to set the mind and taste buds atingle with anticipation, but only for those not suffocated by the stenches of pollution, war, disease and death.

Christmas is bells. Tinkling, caroling, majestic tones, bell-like voices and golden-throated horn-bells proclaim the glory of God in strange renditions of "Happy Birthday, Dear Jesus." But the cries of the hungry, the lonely, the despairing are dissonant notes of cracked bells.

Christmas is love—the Love of God brought to man, love from family and friends, love for those we never knew and love for those we'll meet again. But sometimes hate and humbug harry those who profess this Christmas love.

Christmas is planning and waiting—planning for ways to celebrate the meaning of the season, and waiting for the birthday of the Child who can show us the meaning of the season, and of life; planning and waiting for those who will share our celebrations and waiting, too, for those who cannot come, this time. But some will wait perennially without knowing for Whom they wait.

Christmas is gifts. The richest Gift of all was sent to man, but some refuse delivery. Christmas is sharing abundance with those who have the least and giving to those who are special to us. But some will value more the prices on the stickers so carefully removed.

Christmas is light. Man-made gems gleam against a darkened sky or nest midst verdant boughs. Or glowing candlelights will warm our hearts with their small flames and fill our souls with peace, if we allow. The Light of the world. If only we would press the switch to "On." Never an energy shortage nor need to conserve this Source. But there are those who extinguish the lights of many lives through conflicts and atrocities, and others who seem to prefer the darkness of self-pity.

Christmas is gold and frankincense and myrrh. A golden Life and essence of the Man's words waft strong throughout the world. Breathe deeply, man.

Christmas is birth and rebirth; the birth of a Child who brings the promise of rebirth into a world where it is always Christmas. Gloria!

The holidays near. How shall we confront them? The family in Detroit urges us to spend Christmas there, and doubtless we shall accept. Although some preparations will be the same, we cannot celebrate as before. We originated so many family traditions, but now their re-enactment pains. "Fudge time!" was the cheer that used to start our season.

Thirty pounds, some to give and ample to sample. "You get the spoons; we get the pan" were licking rewards from each session of measuring, melting, grinding and blending confectionery ingredients. During Christmas week, Valeri and Stephen would trudge over snowscapes to deliver greeting plates. Animated and frosty-nosed, they often toted toothsome exchanges from neighbors' kitchens.

Tonight we made the first batch of the year, but the candy-coated spoons and pan were slipped into the dishwater as we finished the chore and skipped the rewards. Perhaps we should stow some traditions in a treasured memory box and unwrap new packages. Maybe E— was right when she suggested it may be unnecessary to continue all our customs. My friend, who listens so often, brings easy closure to concerns that didn't used to pose doubts.

Christmas is anticipation, preparation, decoration, personification, jubilation. Death adds procrastination and evasion.

Like a tot or an expectant mother, I used to be impatient with waiting yet energized by anticipation. Preparation began in early December at my childhood home with decoration of "the tallest tree on the lot" that my Santa was instructed to buy, and every year he would quip, "Where do we cut the hole in the ceiling this year, Mother?"

"Yes, there is a Santa Claus. He lives in the minds and hearts of people," I taught my children, as my mother had, along with the story of a birthday celebration for the Real Reason for jubilation.

Mel and I chose December for our wedding and waited patiently through our second Christmas for Stephen's arrival, which came with the New Year. And how patiently Steve waited, from the Christmas when he learned of our baby-to-be, until the day after Mother's Day when his "wish for a little sister I can make laugh" was granted.

Some years I worked too hard preparing for the festivities. I became ill from shortened sleep and missed meals, got cross from trying to stuff the season like the turkey, cramming it with enough sugarplum memories to last another eleven months. When I got smarter and slowed the frantic pace, I enjoyed it even more.

"Soldiers 'n sailors, firemen and policemen, cowboys 'n Indians" were the sole desires of a four-year-old who was confident Santa would not fail to fill his stocking, while the nearby cookies and milk would satisfy but possibly amplify the good man's middle who helped me comb every toy counter in town for tiny plastic people.

As an uncomplaining and unembarrassed ten-year-old, the same youth waited in a long line with his wary sister until each would perch on one of Saint Nick's knees and she would shyly whisper longings to that jovial, bearded fellow who can both awe and enchant.

This year I wait for Christmas to pass. Three weeks yet. Some shopping is done, but I procrastinate. I weep for Christmas past and lost, except to memory. Yet, that is all they ever are.

I rationalize. This year might have been Steve's last at home for awhile. "It's kinda strange," he wrote, "to be home only during summer or winter." We knew not what assignment he would have after graduation. How lucky to have had twenty-one Christmases and birthdays together. Could we have dreamed last year the nightmare that followed. His last Christmas. Thank God we did not know. Knowing would have been more painful. Is that possible? I know other mothers who feel the same agony this season. And Mary wept not only because man killed a Saviour, but because she lost a Child.

"'Tis the season to be jolly," but the headlines shriek disaster. Stories cry tragedy. Forecasts spell doom.

War
Terrible, Bloody
Shooting, Killing, Dying
Tanks, Guns, Helmets, Bullets
Laughing, Singing, Playing
Beautiful, Lovely
Peace.
STEPHEN LANTZ, GRADE 5

What can we do to change the news? What do God's headlines read? Despair, disenchantment with mortals? Let the birth of the Child bring peace to us this year. It is so hard to find.

Send Christmas cards? What joy had we to circulate? Everyone would understand. Previously, weeks of evenings had been devoted to holiday letters; but to avoid casting a pall, our news had been conveyed this year in summer notes. Later I reconsidered. News from those with whom we only correspond annually was keenly anticipated, and those who had extended the Season of Giving when we most needed to receive must not be slighted. Stephen would want us to say *Good Yule to your family from ours,* so we selected a message revealing our sentiment.

"Christmas
 touches heaven to earth,
 touches heart to heart,
 hand to hand,
 touches sea to shore,
 God to man."
FROM ABBEY PRESS, ST. MEINRAD, INDIANA

The countdown continues. Two weeks now. I had coffee this morning with M— (whose twenty-one year old son was killed in an auto accident). She came from the direction of the

cemetery. Steve's grandmothers regret we buried him so far away. "I'll never see his grave, nor be able to take flowers," each laments. Neither could go to Arlington, and I am sorry to cause more anguish for what seemed an appropriate decision. M— and I talked and cried together because our sons will not be home for Christmas, except in our dreams. The words of that song haunt.

In August of Plebe summer at the Academy, the Sunday evening meal formation in Tecumseh Court had concluded Parents' Weekend. More than twelve hundred members of the Fourth Class stood smartly at attention, a sharp contrast to their crew on I-Day! We would not see them until Christmas leave, its coming touted by their count of months, weeks, days, hours, minutes. Scratch-sounds and static bleared notes blaring from loudspeakers that protruded from windows in Bancroft Hall, the largest dormitory in the world.

> "I'll be home for Christmas
> You can plan on me.
> Please have snow and mistletoe
> And presents on the tree.
> Christmas Eve will find me
> Where the lovelight gleams.
> I'll be home for Christmas
> If only in my dreams."7

Lumps lodged in the throats of Plebe ranks and audience files; but little more than a month later Steve wrote, "I've made a lot of friends, and sometimes feel I've always lived here. This has been a fantastic experience and I'm so glad I came, rather was chosen to come here. Only 102 days 'til Christmas leave. It's great to be alive—and coming home!"

The Firsties' (First Class Midshipmen officer-trainers) musical choice seemed cruel. Its memory is just as cruel. Will you be here, if only in your dreams? Are there dreams in your world? Other songs sadden. I hear Steve's favorites on the radio. I choke on carols. "Hark! The herald angels sing." Is he singing with them?

While Mel and I danced at the office Christmas party, the vocalist asked, ". . . where have all the young men gone?" Such a small opening! Shattered, I fled to the ladies' room for repairs that couldn't be made. "Not ready yet for mascara, I guess," I conceded to Mel's secretary who had retreated with me to lend a shoulder. Weary of pretending merriment, I asked to leave the gathering early.

One week. Preparations wind down. Greetings are in the mail and the house displays a few brave decorations—the crèche, a wreath, the tree. They seem lonely for the rest that hibernate in boxes. Yesterday Mel went to buy the small balsam, a different type placed in a new spot in the family room.

"You guys don't have to have a tree for me; I don't care about one. Besides, we won't even be home for Christmas," Val argued. No one really wanted a tree, but Mel and I suppressed her protest. We would cling to one tradition. However, when purchase day dawned, so did tasks that suddenly couldn't be postponed and headaches. I thought mine to be a classic symptom of grief, but even admitting that probability did not make it leave. Unfair, but Mel shopped alone at a cut-your-own tree farm.

Roaming through rows of acres in sun, rain or snow we always sought the perfect specimen. "Well, nearly perfect," we would compromise, "'cause one side will be against the wall anyway." If the Scotch pine had a flawed silhouette, Mel would prune excess branches from the base, drill the trunk and insert them in the gaps to perfect it. Once, when the perfect tree was the apex of a fifteen-footer, he doggedly sawed with arms elevated overhead, but with less than uplifted thoughts! The ten-foot diameter of that long-needled Austrian pine commandeered the twelve foot width of the living room. Perfect! Thus, we three, then four, annually tramped, chopped, hog-tied and wrestled an oversized porcupine-plant into a groaning station wagon and through restrictive doorways at home.

Tonight as each added an ornament, we did it for the others and, in the process, did not hurt more. No doubt this surprised us all. After the tree was decorated, I looked at the hodgepodge—homemade styrofoam stars and bells from Steve's first

Mickey tree *(How does a two-year-old tongue twist around Christmas?)*; *lopsided papier-mâché stars painstakingly molded by kindergarten fingers;* a shiny, red, glass ball with Stephen in silver glitter script, gift from an elementary teacher; *Valeri's Santa doll;* a large pine cone, each bract exactingly daubed with royal blue sparkles—all quite secure of their status among more elaborate residents.

Lastly, Steve's lighted star has always crowned the top. Val gazed for a long time at the star, too. I wondered what she was thinking. A son became a star to light and inspire, to smile and even laugh about, when we do not remember and weep. Steve's star can light our way, but some days I do not try hard enough to light the way for anyone. *I do not know whether I am too sad, too old, too selfish or all of the above.*

In my thoughts I say, Hello, we love you, *to those who also have family in Stephen's world. Do they hear? Does he? If he does, then he knows the torment of lost communication.* My heart still jumps when the phone rings late at night, but I know that it probably is just a wrong number. I guess he can hear me. I love you Stephen. Good night. I never mail my letters. I don't know your address. Do you read them anyway?

For a while this week everything seemed to go well. The Christmas peace I wished for others enveloped me. Steve seemed to have come home after all. He knew our futile attempts to celebrate and whispered, I understand. It's OK for this year. I love you all.

For one homecoming, Valeri's poster with D and B flags was taped to the garage door, the first thing he would see. Another time she greeted him waving a Navy blue and gold pennant at the airport. Once, when flight connections failed, he drove all night in a rented car, then ninety added miles at 6:00 a.m. to return the one-way auto to its distributor. He reached home exhausted yet exhilarated just to be there.

Christmas or not, Steve's seabag was always stuffed like Santa's with knickknacks or presents. How many rainbow ropes of plastic beads from Mardi Gras we found in the boxes from the Academy, and even my birthday card purchased far ahead! But we miss most his gift of self. Sometimes it seems he gave much more than he received.

After Grandma died, Mother said, "I lost my best friend." Mother is a best friend, too, and I shall miss her sorely when her time comes. Now I know a best friend can be a son or daughter, spouse, parent or friend. But our Best Friend never leaves.

Mel and I shared tears and handclasps in church on our anniversary while all the carols and memories pulsed from mind to heart to hand a hundred times. J— and M— took us, and we were grateful not to sit alone. Valeri stayed home with a migraine. Perhaps she needed more solitary time as Christmas draws ever nearer.

Christmas Eve in Detroit. Valeri and I wept after she returned from her cousins' school pageant. I cried not for her brother, but because my beloved daughter was suffering. Later, Mother cried in my arms as I sat on her bed after everyone had gone to sleep; and we reminisced, like long ago when I was home. And my dad, of stoic Scandinavian genes but tender heart, sobbed as our arms encircled early Christmas morning before the others came downstairs. The fortitude we shammed before others surrendered to emotional defeat.

Many praise me for my courage. Don't praise me. Cry with me and mine who also face the world with outward calm while turmoil rages within. "It's useless to cry about that which you can do nothing," I used to emphasize. Yet, crying continues as from an open flood gate. Once tears have flowed, though, comes another armistice with grief.

As gifts were unwrapped, we cheerily cried out our old reminder to "Save the bows!" Should I also save the feelings of the past two days? Still, moments of merriment peeked out valiantly from shrouded hearts determined not to fall part.

It is finished. We are home. As I look at Steve's portrait on the bookcase shelf I know he is gone, but still await the call that he's coming. "I'll be on United flight — —, arriving at 2033 for all you military types. That's 8:33 for you civilians; and for you Marines, Mickey's big hand is on. . . . !" It is we who are on stand-by flights to his destination, and he awaits our arrivals. I wish God ran better schedules for families. Our layovers are too long.

In the mail were letters from Paula's mother and Pat's parents who also struggle with these days, and one from the motel confirming Graduation Week reservations that we had made during Parents Weekend. Not so, my friends. Our son was graduated with full honors last spring, ahead of his class, to a more challenging duty, another alumni association. And in J— and D—'s letter was a poem by Henry Van Dyke, another parent who wrote of mourning and healing after the death of his twenty-four year old daughter.

> "A deeper crimson in the rose
> A deeper blue in sky and sea
> And ever, as the summer goes,
> A deeper loss in losing thee!
> A deeper music in the strain
> Of hermit-thrush from lonely tree;
> And deeper grows the sense of gain
> My life has found in loving thee.
> A deeper love, a deeper rest,
> A deeper joy in all I see
> And ever deeper in my breast
> A silver song that comes from thee."

Mel and Valeri took down the tree tonight. I cared not at all that we took it away early, just as I cared not that we decorated it late. It mattered not that we often seemed without spirit. Actually we were not without. Either the spirit lay dormant or the winds of sorrow blowing through our minds slammed the door in its face when it tried to enter.

"Learn to use Stephen's life and love as a stepping stone into the future, not as a boulder in your way as you again seek love in life" was advice to Paula from her chaplain. If tomorrow we step into tranquility, will we know happiness? If we don't find it, we can hypnotize ourselves to believe it, drift with the tides of life and stay afloat. Some might call this a trip!

Throughout these months friends have shored us, but some I thought to be friends have ignored. Yet, I have learned not to be disappointed. My door is still open to those who did not learn of Steve's death until long afterward and now believe it too late to call or write, so others tell me. "I cannot face her now." Now is not ever. And I am sorry for some who avoided us because, as friends, they could not bear their grief and ours.

A multitude steadied us, brightened our journey through the season like luminaria lighting our way. I hope they know how well they succeeded. We knew Christmas Blessing. Did we doubt at times we would? I did. We talked out the old year without tears. Even now I write without them. A new beginning?

1 January, the beginning of a new decade. Tomorrow would have been beginnings for Steve, too—his 22nd birthday, the countdown toward graduation and another chapter after commissioning.

It is not enough to cope with the anxieties of death. Coping does nothing to resolve problems, create directions or fire dreams. When we can do these things again, we can gain something we didn't even realize we missed. I wish to make a new beginning to this year, decade, remainder of my life with resolution, enthusiasm and peace of mind. Wishing will not make it so; but I am as a young woman again, seeking identity. I found it once. Shall I find it again? Do we seek more answers after death has touched us?

Books are the only friends that don't object to being used. Since childhood I have leaned on them for recreation, education, inspiration and consolation. I liken them to our lives, each major event a chapter, each person a character to shape our story. Some are long, others seem unfortunately abbreviated. Books continued as my companions through grief, too; but I swapped escapes through fiction for self-repair manuals of enlightenment—the Scriptures, poetry and essays.

In The Winter Beach *I see the panorama: evolution, survival, perpetuity—relentless cycles of life and death. Timelessness. No dates on which to peg a dream. "The confrontation of the sea by the land is like life's confrontation with eternity—that eternity we all look on every moment, whether consciously or not. . . . High time I made myself accessible to whatever instruction might be gained on that momentous frontier. . . ."*[8]

I yearn for the sea of our lives to be unchanging. How foolish. It always has calms and storms. Death confronted us so powerfully that we were forced to confront eternity head on. But beyond a daily existence, I cannot embrace a life fragmented by sorrow. I am disappointed in myself. Where is blind faith, sometimes the only answer? Oh, Stephen you seem so far away. Oh, God, I seem so far away.

2 January. Stephen's birthday. We flew the flag. It flew at half-mast at the Academy during the week after he died. "I just wish the people of this country would feel as much pride in America as I do. But then, not everyone is as fortunate as I," he once wrote. On the altar we placed flowers today "dedicated to the glory of God and in loving memory of the birthday of Stephen C. Lantz." We should have added with thanksgiving. And at Arlington, Paula's parents wrote they have removed from Steve's grave the small Christmas tree they had trimmed. Bizarrely, his birthday was celebration. G— sent us a birthday card; Pat's mother called from Texas; the librarian phoned to say a memorial book was being placed in circulation; Brian invited himself to spend the evening with the parents of his best friend; and Val typed a gift.

"I'll lend you for a little time
    a child of mine," He said.
'For you to love the while he lives,
    and mourn for when he's dead.
It may be six or seven years
    or twenty-two or three.
But will you, 'til I call him back,
    take care of him for me?
He'll bring his charms to gladden you
    and should his stay be brief,
You'll have his lovely memories
    as solace for your grief.
I cannot promise he will stay
    since all from earth return;
But there are lessons taught down there
    I want this child to learn.
I've looked the wise world over
    in search of teachers true
And from the throngs that crowd life's loves,
    I have selected you.
Now will you give him all your love,
    nor think the labor vain
Nor hate me when I come to call
    to take him back again?
I fancied that I heard them say,
    'Dear Lord, Thy will be done.
For all the joy Thy child shall bring,
    the risk of grief we'll run.
We'll shelter him with tenderness,
    we'll love him while we may.
But should the angels call for him
    much sooner than we'd planned
We'll brave the bitter grief that comes
    and try to understand.'" AUTHOR UNKNOWN

God must have given children to parents to demonstrate the truest meaning of love. Yet I read of pressured parents driven mad enough to abuse. Time heals, they say. Can time heal the guilt of torture perpetrated on innocents? What parents whose child has died has sympathy or forgiveness for one who has wasted one? If we are not to judge, surely we do cry for justice in our outrage. And then we ask for understanding and compassion.

Today is the first, truly wintry day. The wind howls cold and swirls snow around the house like dancing veils. Frenzied crystals whirl and jostle to and fro in disorganized choreography, finally tumbling to the ground in exhausted heaps. Lord, let us not live in this fashion.

Do you have weather in your world? I think not, for the atmosphere where souls reside surely must be constantly pleasant. Perhaps we come to earth to experience weather for awhile! Tomorrow I begin a new year at the hospital. Who is sick and who is dying? Who cares, and who is caring? A year ago Steve clipped his horoscope from the paper. "A more exciting you will emerge this coming year. You can expect to become more active, more communicative," it said in part. I contemplate another meaning to those words as I am aware of the influence his life continues to have.

"Before I met Steve, he was described to me as the model midshipman, one I should try to copy. In charge of my, and other Plebes' professional development, he was Mr. Lantz, Sir. He explained things so that you felt as if you arrived at the answer. His attitude was contagious and I found myself getting as excited about ships and planes as he. I remember when he first spooned me—allowed me to call him by his first name. I looked at him as an older brother. I feel positive Steve is in heaven; and now I have a friend there who can help me, just like he used to."

Dear Steve. Can you move through time and space? Is everyone happy there? Is living taught better? What problems do you solve? Are they beyond our understanding? So many undecipherables.

"... You would know the secret of death.
But how shall you find it unless you
seek it in the heart of life?
... For life and death are one, even as
the river and the sea are one.

In the depths of your hopes and desires
lies your silent knowledge of the beyond;
And like seeds dreaming beneath the snow
your heart dreams of spring. . . .

And what is it to cease breathing, but to
face the breath from its restless tides,
that it may rise and expand and
seek God unencumbered?

... And when you have reached the mountain top,
then you shall begin to climb,
And when the earth shall claim your limbs,
then shall you truly dance."[9]

My answers? Patience, faith and curiosity—but don't just sit there while you're waiting!

Tonight I watch Boots snoozing on his rug and remember when Steve and I drove to the kennel for that puppy. I never really wanted a dog, but he was my promise, kept. Steve's own. His elation could scarcely be contained in that eight-year-old frame. He has left us his pet, our burden now. But we shall not want to lose that complaining old mutt; and when he dies, we shall be sad for his leaving, for the reminder that he was Steve's. And we'll realize that a part of our son has died again.

"Don't let my plants die while I'm gone," he had cautioned. One day soon I must replant the mallard (planter he had for eleven years). Its plant is flourishing, but the ivy in the boy (planter) looks sick. It is as if I should be especially careful to preserve these lives.

After high school Stephen mused, "It's ironic. I'm the first of my friends to leave home, but I'm not nearly as eager as most of them. I would be perfectly content to stay here until I'm thirty-five, if I could accomplish some other things I want to do." "Oh, no, you don't," I retorted. "You've gotta get out of here before then so you can get a job and support us in our old age!"

How I wish he could have stayed here, if only until thirty-five. I miss our all-night raps; for now I am alone, not only when I write, but when I try to communicate to Mel. He says I am still too melancholy. He wishes my grief were also buried at Arlington. It will not die, let alone be buried. Wishing will not make it happen. There is no cure, yet, just symptomatic relief. Like a virus, grief must run its course; and some of us will be afflicted longer.

I love the loneness of night. Cacaphony of radio, TV, conversation annoys sometimes, competes with softer voices from within. I cannot share with those who are closest now. one with whom I could is gone.

Normally solid, our marriage floundered through grief; but even the healthiest of relationships can be injured when a common calamity befalls two who also are best friends. Their hurt may press each to become more private or to be uncomfortable being alone together; their aptitude for listening and understanding may be blunted.

Mel says I must change my nighttime routine. I don't know if I can, or should. At least in this pattern I can function during the day. If I'm not made to feel guilty or strange because of lingering grief, I shall recuperate. I try to reach out to him, but am misunderstood or rebuffed. So I shall try with someone else, or maybe quit. We lash out at those we least want to hurt, and ask for understanding; but they cannot help because they have shortcomings like ours, or others of their own.

Mel says he cannot tolerate stress at home because his job is stressful. True, but so is mine. Of that he's not convinced. Talking is catharsis for me, brings new pain to him. He says he cannot talk late evening; but there's little other time, so he escapes to the lake to fish, the field to walk, the workshop to grieve alone. Then I escape into depression and each walks a treadmill going nowhere to recovery. So we bring little to the other but a salary, an evening meal, clean clothes, scant moments of pleasure. It's not enough. I have suggested we seek someone of his choice to discuss our problems. More avoidance or delay. Perhaps time will bring change for the better. But I feel that, in his eyes, mine has nearly run out.

A winternight from my window: Silhouettes of naked trees hover near clumps of boxes; smoke spectres drift, dissipate grey vastness. Moon beacons caress the earth stilled beneath a crystalline counterpane. Anger cools. Frustrations end their tumbling. I am lulled to sleep and peace.

For several years Valeri had explored drama through classes and roles with our community youth theater. Twenty-five years earlier, greasepaint had enticed me to join a local players' group, but continued participation was sidetracked by more interests than time. This winter when she auditioned for a Civic Players production, I spontaneously bid for the role of the mother. Unfamiliar with the play, I envisioned her as a somewhat stereo-typical parent-figure, for which I felt qualified to read. Only after first callbacks for *Ladyhouse Blues* did I read the entire script in which *the family has lost its only twenty-year old son to disease while he was serving in the U.S. Navy!*

What lured me to that tryout? No, audition, our director insists. "Cheerleaders try out. And, doctors and lawyers practice; we shall rehearse." Why didn't I read the script until after callbacks when, by then, my appetite was whetted? Why didn't I reject the part when it was offered and I did know the story line? What possibly can come from this venture? I have discussed doubts with others.

"What will people think?"
"Do whatever you want, what you feel you can do."
"If the role is offered and you accept, you'll do a good job."
"I think Steve would want me to do it."
"Steve would be so proud of you."
"Why do you want to put yourself through all that again?"
"I don't look at it that way."

How do I look at it then? A chance to be in a play again; a challenge for my acting ability, if I have any; something new and fun. Needed! I can learn something. How I can learn—lines!

There are problems within the script for me to deal with, sooner or later. That is the question—early or later? On stage or in my life? Supposedly all problems are prettied with gift wrap. What greater problem for a parent than to have a child die? That gift we do not need.

The mother and I are kindred—sometimes stubborn, unreasonable, uncomplicated; tender beneath a shell of self-sufficiency, seldom asking for help; bearing grief strongly, some say.

At rehearsal tonight I could only start to read the son's last letter. A postponement of the scene was granted, unquestioned. No one but Val knows my conflict. I hope not to burden the director, cast or crew, for I want to do this role well. I almost feel a calling. Is it imagined? I want to say what's inside, relate to the audience.

After one difficult rehearsal, I voiced uncertainties to Val who worked the light crew and became light board operator for the performances. "I dare not break down on stage so that the role is endangered. If I lose lines because of personal emotion, it will be disastrous. I'll not only make a fool of myself, but spoil that show. It must not happen."

"No way," she replied, nonchalantly adding, "You won't. But just remember if you do, I'll throw a blackout on ya'!" Her radical solution didn't have to be effected. Maybe the threat countered my trepidation. What a fate for any actor!

Excessive consumption of caffeine, coupled with the tension I attempted to manage, caused several bouts of arrhythmia. My coffee cup was shelved; and when the final curtain rang down, my symptoms joined it. During the run, however, my pen was not idle.

Nine months. Stephen has been gone as long as I carried him. There were times in both spans when it seemed more like nine years, or ninety.

We try to remain involved with life, anesthetize raw edges that sting without analgesics. Elixirs. Over-the-counters or over-coffees. Prescriptions. We imbibe any accessible remedy, but still OD at times on grief.

Happy Valentine's Day, Steve. I missed sending a Care package, and not only this month. I should send to others, but I did call Paula and am pleased she wants to come for the play.

While packing for his first year at the Academy, Steve wondered whether or not to include some items. "Never mind," I commented. "I can always send them with your Care packages."

"Care packages? I always thought those were for needy people somewhere."

"Well, college students have needs, but actually the parcels are just to say 'Hi, we care!'"

Later he wrote, "Mail from home is like the fresh breeze that blows from the Severn. Oh, yes, we can have food in our rooms, so Care packages will be more than welcomed." And it was bonanza-ville when three *roomies* received parcels the same week!

Every day I run lines (of the play). On the table beside me sits Great-grandma's clock, ticking and tolling, endless ticks and tones telling seconds, minutes, hours, decades. I never knew Great-grandmother Johnson, but I have her clock which marked her long years. Why couldn't it have chimed longer for Steve? He was already at Annapolis when Dad gave it to us; but Steve had another family timepiece, Grandpa's pocket watch. He even bought a uniform vest so he could wear it. The watch didn't tick long for him either. "My old grandfather's watch *sits alone in the drawer. . . . But it stopped, short, never*

to go again, when the young man died." When the watch was returned from the Academy, I could not make it run again.

The script is learned, the role developed through countless rehearsals. The curtain goes up on a vignette of life. Repeat the dialogue, feel interaction, move with a mood, bask in accolades, bind with new kin, cope with unforeseens, differ with reviews. The curtain rings down on a tableau of players frozen in a vignette. Now, emptiness. Lean against the best Support and ask for comfort, for the thousandth time.

Comfort comes from the rhythm of Steve's march through our lives, his tempo and theme. March again with us as we continue across our parade grounds, down our streets. Like the mother, I talk to God and a loved one in "the Eternal," and they listen to me if I have anything to tell them.

Paula came to live in our community for awhile. After coming to see a performance of *Ladyhouse Blues*, she had an opportunity for a job interview. Because the position was available immediately, her decision to relocate was precipitous. Within a few days she moved seven hundred miles to our home, began her new employment and started assembling furnishings for her first apartment, a small condominium which Mel and I decided to purchase with a portion of Stephen's insurance money.

I don't want Val to become jealous of our endeavors for Paula. I realized she may be when she lashed out at me tonight (about my time spent with Paula) and I to her. She must not believe we loved Steve more than her, now shown in what we do for Paula. Val has lost one she adored. I wish Paula could become her confidante, a sister friend. Paula would be a natural, if Val accepts. But that (relationship) must not be a burden to Paula. It won't. She is close to her own sisters and could include Val, too, I feel sure. Dear God, let both find peace, hope and happiness again. Listen to Mom, dear Son. You help, too.

Although Steve and Paula had been engaged and home visits exchanged, distance curtailed interacting between the families. Her unforeseen relocation with us brought a kinship with the

C—'s that would change direction but not end when she later returned east.

Winter is long, this season of my discontent.

Dear Stephen,

Tonight I think about our last days together and know guilt. Forgive me. I never said *Goodbye* so finally to anyone before.

You asked me twice the question I didn't want to hear: Am I dying? I hedged in answering. Do we always hope against hope? When does a family acknowledge death together and find strength? The final day. We needed to give you strength earlier, face truth together; but we did not, or could not. Whom did we protect with that unspoken decision? Sometimes I think your not knowing depressed you more. Or did you know? You must have. Don't they say the dying know?

I could talk easily with those who came that last day. But I was a coward not to tell you things deep in my heart, one last time. I was already numbed. The one person I most wanted to comfort on 13 May I failed. Others spoke for me. I hope you're hearing my words now.

You might have liked communion; we four could have shared that. You would have liked the Midshipman's Prayer, and the chaplain could have recited it. Your lips could have mouthed the words as they did with Paula's songs. You and I talked about climbing a tough mountain. I should have said I was climbing with you and that we might see God at the summit; but my voice didn't even get there.

I know you have infinite knowledge now. I'm sure you understand my weakness now. I wish this conversation were not one way. Until we can share speech and hearing again, Shalom.

Love always,
Mom

Aboard a ship,
adrift at times through life;
then I set sail for
new worlds,
adventure.
But the wind comes up and
tosses me about.
My vessel leaks.
I bail and pray,
furiously,
ride out the storm.
Tears or
salt spray on my face?
No matter which,
they cloud my sight,
shroud my hope.
The boat has sprung a leak!
I'm sinking!
It does not happen,
Nor do the angry winds
capsize my craft.

Spring

*"Learn to grow and change in the present
And to let the past go gently."* AUTHOR UNKNOWN

"Greetings from Canoe U., that amazing Academy famous for its ferocious frigate captains," Stephen penned during the spring of Plebe Year. "The weather is beautiful. I'm playing tennis well. The winter-guard, D and B color guard, are fine and my grades are good. How could I ask for more?" But an academic bête-noire, one's pet aversion, could temper his perspective. "After this week your son may be radioactive from being nuked by the physics exam." An innocent foreshadow.

A year ago today, the beginning of the end, Paula had picked up Steve for midterm break. Dear Paula. What a lovely daughter you would have been. I feel cheated, and cheated out of those grandchildren we shall not have. She and Steve must have felt cheated, too.

He wasn't feeling well that day. How sick he was! Would that we could have known then. Would that anyone could have helped later. Did he suspect? No matter. Everyone knew too soon.

Prior to Bethesda, Paula and Stephen had weighed the possibility of a malignancy, even his death. "Are you afraid to die?" she asked.

"No, I'm not afraid. I'm not ready to go, yet; but I'm not afraid."

At Bethesda Valeri overheard his telephone chat with friends at home. "I'm dying, you know." His matter-of-fact appraisal was abruptly amended. "Just kidding," he mumbled after hearing their horrified remonstrances. And Mel would never forget Steve's poignant forewarning the night he was transferred to the ICU as Valeri and I remained to secure his room. "Take care of Mom and Val." Did he already know what we later surmised but kept submerged?

For how long did he retain confidence like he once had written to his grandmother after her emergency surgery? "I know you'll be fine. I put my trust in God and the doctors." Or, unlike the optimism in a junior high composition, during his illness did he realize that he had run out of wishes?

"If a genie granted me three wishes, I would wish for an end to nuclear weaponry, a worldwide agreement to protect wildlife, and all the wishes I wanted. The first two are for obvious reasons; but, with the third, I could go back in time, or wish for an end to the world's problems. Who knows? I might wish to become a world ruler. Naturally, this is a big responsibility; but if I ever got into hot water, I would have another wish to get me out!"

March 15, the Ides of March, dated Stephen's last letter to his grandparents: "Did pretty well on mid-terms. Don't know if I'll keep my stars next semester but, at this point, that's the least of my worries. Until this whole mess, I was in charge of coordinating summer training programs for about five hundred in our Battalion. Here's a scoop! During second set of Plebe summer training, I will be D and B Corps Commander. That's the guy who stands in front of everybody and looks like he's shooing away flies. He attempts to tell the Plebes where to go. Hippity-Ho, Corps, Go! Hippity-Hop, Corps, Stop! Well, that's about all from the sickie."

Little more than two months until the Storm. I should not remind myself so often of the date, but Val and I checked the calendar today for her birthday. Mother's Day this year. What sadness. What joy. I do not know if I can handle both emotions. It is so unfair to Val that her important day be tied to tragedy. Will it always be? One prayer was granted me at Bethesda: he did not die on her birthday. Maybe in the future the scars will harden, but then the day will not be Val's Sixteenth.

Lent: introspection, self-denial, repentance. If we knew what awaited our lives, we might be born crying, My God, why hast Thou forsaken me? But on longer observation we might correct that to say, How great Thou art! "In small proportions we just beauties see, and in short measure life may perfect be." (Ben Jonson) The promise of Easter. Even if faith in eternal life is strong, faith must eternally be renewed. To Stephen at Easter, the only Care package I can send this year:

> Birth, a miracle.
> A son awaited,
> nurtured, flourished,
> served, departed,
> alive yet in
> deathless memory.
> Birth, the miracle.
> The Son awaited. . . .

Care packages are not restricted to brown paper wrappings with strapping tape. In a small white envelope, an unknown woman jotted a note to me. "I saved your son's obituary to remind me that other mothers, every day, suffer excruciating losses. At the time I cut it out, I was thinking of the death of one of my own sons. I did not know that I would find occasion to extend my sympathy and tell you how meaningful your lines [of dialogue] were. My grandmother had the strength which the mother and you, Norma, display. I gain strength from such women. May this late fan letter cheer your day." She and I knew the truth of one line from *Ladyhouse Blues:* "That boy had love in him . . . We got to hang onto that . . . ."[10] Enclosed in her letter was a selection from Wordsworth which she had dedicated to her son in the newspaper Memorials.

> "We will grieve not, rather find
> Strength in what remains behind;
> In the primal sympathy
> Which having been must ever be;
> In the soothing thoughts that spring
> Out of human suffering;
> In the faith that looks through death;
> In years that bring the philosophic mind."

Daily I read vital statistics. Who are arriving? Births. Who are new? Marriages. Who are leaving? Divorces, Deaths. How old are they? I am drawn to the ages of those who have died and feel compassion, or is it morbid comfort, to learn our family is not alone in its loss of a young family member? I read Memorials among the Obituaries. Twenty years sometimes do others grieve. Such a long time. But who is to judge, and who to measure the length of heartbreak?

Some Care parcels have feet. "Sunday I helped with the Special Olympics at our track. This is a really big thing and I'm glad I could help," Steve wrote. In another letter, "Today I'm going to make a donation at the bloodmobile. It comes to the Academy every Tuesday and midshipmen are encouraged to participate."

R— called to say she had taxied to Arlington while in D.C. for her conference. Such a special effort. I wish I could go again. I never could understand the need or desire of people who continue visiting cemeteries, unless perhaps for genealogy or history, as we have done.

Along the Mississippi, prehistoric Americans sculpted monumental mounds of earth into effigies of bird and bear to harbor their dead; but stalwart settlers rest beside their less illustrious contemporaries, like Blackbeard, under unnamed and ill-famed sounds, salt marshes or the parched sands of countless coasts. Some Founding Fathers sleep in ornate plantation crypts or sepulchers in Philadelphia; but in a more humble graveyard with their pioneer parents lay eight children named Baby Boy or Girl, perished either in emigration from their common womb or victims of hostile organisms of the cruel land which reclaimed them before the circuit preacher came to christen.

Now as we drive by a cemetery, no one jests, "There's a marble orchard."

"Oh, that's the place people are just dying to get in." I still don't understand all the why's of visiting cemeteries, only know the urge to return, where I gain serenity among those in absolute repose.

Tonight Valeri brought out photo albums and we looked at snapshots, but no one continued for long. After she and Mel were asleep, I brought them out again to recapture earlier years, happier times. What we were shows in our faces. We do not take pictures anymore. Our lives seem so torn now. Will we ever know the same joie de vivre? Was it as we remember, or do we imagine it better than it was? Like "the Easter you'll never forget, Steve."

That's Loo-ray, Dad!" Val thrilled when we spotted lights winking, as if from low stars, on the dark mountainside ahead. Splendors of the Lurary Caverns were as unforgettable as another moment of that vacation on Easter evening along the Blue Ridge Parkway.

The first picnic of the season climaxed our hike among dogwood-whitened slopes. Leaving Valeri with twigs to nudge a nascent flame, Stephen and I searched separately, but on parallel paths, for larger wood while Mel returned to the car for our food. Hiking above me, Steve flushed an unseen animal. Startled, it trampled brush with abandon as it crashed across my trail that curved downhill, just out of sight. Halting,

I measuredly backed up the incline, hallooing for Stephen to join me. Together we cautiously approached the resumed, noisy foraging. Concluding it came from a bear and realizing Val's vulnerability, we beat a retreat to the picic spot.

Informing Mel but not her of our near encounter, we opted to stay, protected by our babel and crackling fire. As twilight deepened, however, we could scarcely compete with the clamor from the woodland's restless natives.

"What are all those sounds?" Val asked throughout supper.

"Raccoons, most likely, and other animals."

"Like bears?" she insisted, who, although young, was no novice to the outdoors.

"Umm, probably deer, badgers, small creatures."

"And bears?" she persevered.

"Oh, . . . well maaay-be, but nothing's going to bother us with this blaze going."

Realizing we needed water to extinguish the campfire before we left, Stephen grabbed the thermos jug to fill from the pump a few hundred yards away. He sauntered off, whistling in the dark.

Valeri fretted. "What if there are bears out there? What if Brother gets lost?"

"Oh, we'll come back to look for him when it's daylight," we teased. Another witticism provoked laughter.

He whooped, "Hey, you guys. This isn't funny. I think there's a bear near!"

"Head for the car, Steve," Mel yelled as we raced up the grade to his aid, stumbling over roots and stumps that lurked in shadows beyond the firelight. We reached our steel refuge just as Steve, behind the open car door, flicked the headlights to spotlight a large, blinking bear!

Driving to the well, he explained, "I was jogging along when I heard something padding behind me, keeping up; and it didn't sound like anyone in tennis shoes! I realized the smell of hot dogs on my unwashed hands probably invited it to find the source. It didn't take long for me to figure out it was a bear, and that's when I got movin'."

All were relieved that he had not become a dinner host to that finger-lickin' guest! And Val had her day in court: "I told you guys so!"

The first warm, spring weekend. Mel and I worked on the new porch and in the yard. As I weeded and edged the beds, I saw how much of Stephen is here—his plants from last May, to be sure, but also the brick walls, sidewalk and the garden swing he and Mel built during more than one spring; the sticky, summer hours he spent among the raspberries for bonuses of pies. The cactus bloomed again this year. With pocketknife and rock, Mel and he had pried it from the sun-parched wilds of South Dakota for my new (plant) collection; but it never bloomed until the year he died.

*Earth awakes.
The soil is warmed
anew.
Clouds pledge rain
to quicken life
into the sleeping.*

*Plants arouse,
a drowsy press to grow
again.
With mindless set,
probing tips
seek light and air.*

*Birds resume
their journeys home,
afar.
Impelled to move,
they need to ready
distant nests.*

*Spring's rhythmic zest
and man is blest—
Re-genesis.*

Today I visited a young man at the hospital who lay sleeping, pale from mono. A special friend sat with him and I chatted with her. I did not want to waken him, nor did I really want to talk with him. Another young man slept in the bed beside his. Do all young men in the hospital look so vulnerable? It was I, today, who was so vulnerable.

While I was gardening, a young neighbor came to introduce her first-born. Watching her beaming face as she tenderly pulled aside the blanket to show the dozing infant, I thought about my own emotional high twenty-one years before. My stammered apology tripped over the heels of my congratulations as I scurried indoors to avoid overexposure, but not from the sun.

Paula played her guitar and sang for a few moments this evening and then went downstairs to sand furiously on her table. We have worked hard to finish everything so she can move into her apartment this weekend. Keeping busy is good. As their birthdays near, she and Valeri must be reliving silently the agony of a year ago. The changes in all our lives within three of their birthdays blow my mind.

"How many children do you have?" raises the most discrepant replies. If I answer my preference, *two,* and the acquaintance is aware of but one, an inquiry logically follows. "Oh, where is your other?"

If someone sees Steve's picture in our home, he may observe, "I didn't realize you have a son in the Navy."

"He attended the Naval Academy."

"What a marvelous opportunity! Where is he now?"

Any response brakes conversation. But I shall not put away his picture. I rebel against *passed away,* nor did I *lose* him anywhere. If only others were not discomposed by "We have two children, a daughter and a son who died."

I counted back, one year minus three weeks that Steve's voice came over the phone with the worst news we would ever hear. I try to live each day with some positivity; but how shall we face this Mother's Day, this 13 May?

Tonight I mull scraps gleaned from somewhere: "The whole theory of the universe comes down to one life, one day at a time."

"Life is like an onion. You peel off one layer at a time." Yes, and sometimes you cry.

"We shape our lives not by what we carry with us, but by what we leave behind."

May Day! May Day! Steve's was a year ago when the disease blighted his lungs. It's my May Day, too, all over again. "Why me?" Steve asked and I can but echo dumbly, Why him? Gradually, insidiously, methodically, reality creeps into my mind: as long as I live, I shall not see Stephen again. The fact comes stealthily, on cat's paws, like a lightning bolt, or as the gnawing persistence of pleurisy; but tears don't stream as often now, nor as long. Some say Steve would not want our continuing tears. Yet, were he the one left, I think he might have felt death so. Two days ago we took Paula's parents to see the Bennington flag[F] and learned another copy of the Academy history also had been donated there. What we leave behind.

Mother's Day. Bart and Charla called to say they are to be married in August in the Academy Chapel. How I hope we can go. Val's birthday today. She did not want to plan a party as before, but yesterday we surprised her with lunch at a restaurant with her friends. She seemed truly happy. Today the family emphasized her day which helped us swallow more easily the bitter sips, reminders.

After she left to spend the night with Paula (they became very close), the phone rang and Mel was urged to report to work. In shock and disbelief I heard him agree to go. After my anger and tears he stayed home, and one more crisis in our relationship is temporarily averted. I cannot know for how long. I cannot know his allegiance. Our love is being consumed by a cancer. We treat the symptoms, but do not give it our biggest guns; and I do not know if we shall reach remission or a cure.

13 May, at 4:05 P.M. our clocks stopped. Another storm came into our lives on this anniversary of Stephen's death. A tornado dealt death, injury and destruction from west to east across our town!

When Mel dashed in the back door minutes earlier, we scanned the sky for the funnel he thought he had spotted. Nearly on us, its tail snaked and lashed across the neighbors' yards. "I think we'd better go to the basement, right now!" Frozen to his rug, stubborn Boots would not go, so Val carried him.

Ma Bell's usual timing. Just as we reached the foot of the stairwell, the telephone rang. Across town, a friend of Valeri's who had heard the warning sirens was home alone. "Val, what should I do?"

"Take your puppies and go to the basement."

"What then?"

"Get under something. Take cover. Look, I really can't talk right now. We're having a tornado here!"

The pressure dropped. Ears popped. Whooshes, like giant lariats. Loud thuds. Silence. Pressure returned. What had happened upstairs? Smoke gently floated down the hall. A fire? No, thankfully, just plaster dust. Then, the realization as we looked at each other: we had survived a tornado!

Another telephone summons! Alerted by the radio, our next-door neighbor called from work to learn the extent of damages; but we were unable to report details and rang off seconds before the phone went dead.

Our bedroom was air-conditioned by two gaping holes in the west wall. The dresser mirror, Grandma's cane chair, the whatnot shelf — demolished. Two-by-eights (from the Mormon Church) had slammed about capriciously, puncturing walls *and ceiling with the force of a catapult. "Not very Christian of you!" I later teased J— (my Mormon neighbor). One sixfoot section lay next to the bed; overhead, the other half had pierced the ceiling like an arrow. Shards of glass peppered and punctured the bedspread, studded the wall behind the headboard of the bed. Fortunate for Mel and me, the time had not been arrested at 4:05 A.M.*

A section of one timber slid across the hall into Val's room where it had come to rest amid more debris and dust. "Ah, well, on occasion I have said your room looks like a tornado struck it." "Mother!" her indignant retort. Insulation, glass, woodbits, plaster everywhere. One chunk near the stove thirty feet away. A chair fragment in the dining room. Only things.

Outside, grim. Live lines down. Gas lines broken. Gross destruction less than three hundred feet away. Where were our friends and neighbors?

E—, her husband and daughter were on vacation in Kentucky, but where was their son whom I had seen jog by less than an hour before? Across the street from theirs, H—'s house was nearly leveled. Where were she and her two babies? Her children had napped at the sitter's, outside the neighborhood, because she had been called into work unexpectedly.

No warning sirens.[G] *Dazedly people began to move about. "Where were you when it hit?" Heads shook in disbelief. Some cried. Shock. Dismay. Relief. Though late afternoon, a long day had begun. In my kitchen the Bunyanesque pot of soup bubbling on a back burner would dispense respite from refuse.*

Near midnight I noted the time. I have thought of Steve often these eight hours. There was no time for remorse, but we felt him here. Still framed in the cut crystal and brass Christmas gift from Valeri, and perching on the end of my dresser, Steve seemed to watch serenely from the sole exposed, unscathed item in the room.

Outside, the utility crews toiled through the night: securing gas lines and water pipes, tying off and repairing electric lines, restoring communication with those outside our cordoned, police-patrolled streets. Dark figures with flashlights and ID's roamed the yards, made house checks, inquired after the needs of candle-bearing residents. The eerie atmosphere was stifling; I virtually felt imprisoned. After 2:00 a.m., I fell into sleep troubled by an exhausted body and mind that already planned tomorrows of sifting shambles for salvage—again.

At 3:00 the phone rang! Dashing to answer before it awakened the others, I muttered a choice expletive. On the line was E— in Kentucky, whose geographer-husband had recognized our devastated neighborhood from aerial photographs telecast nationally. Attempting to reach us for hours through jammed telephone circuits, she had but one question: "Where is our son?"

"He's safe, asleep right now in Steve's bed with Abbey (their dog). Do you want me to get him?"

"No, thank God. Did it hit our house?"

"Afraid so."

"What's the bad news?"

Pause. More than time to gather thoughts, a pause pillows a hard answer. What should I tell them? Eight rooms on two floors are ankle deep in glass and rubble? Most furnishings are unsalvageable? We have boarded all windows with plywood to forestall bad weather, or vandals? Your house fared better than your neighbor's which is roofless, the second story gutted even of clothes from all the closets?

"It's a real disaster, but you will be able to repair it. Mel says it's structurally sound. Just be prepared for a lot of wreckage. The important thing is that G— and Abbey are OK."

> Much to be done. Many new chapters to begin. I hope the tornado can finish a chapter for Mel and me. We must sweep out shattered dreams, battered thoughts, sharp words, and repair splintered emotions. We need to build a stronger bridge over our troubled waters, for the old one sometimes sways dangerously in the winds of misunderstanding and selfishness. Our bedroom is damaged, but there is much of significance there, still undestroyed. Are there messages to be read on the dusty furniture-faces of our home? We have survived this long. Perhaps we can regain the love we once knew. Yet, que será, será. Lord, help us to give love without strings, guidance without dogmatism, support without only if's.

The tornado inflicted deep distress, not only on those whose relatives and friends fell victim to injury or death, but among a larger number who felt themselves buried by the refuse of shattered homes, possessions and lifestyles. As they labored through months of disruption and construction, I saw their grief: anger that it happened, denial that it did, depression from the apparently insurmountable reordering, physical ailments and exaggerated emotions that hindered their progress. But like the intrepid plants that elbowed aside and swarmed over the shrapnel of building materials that had blitzed their beds, so people reclaimed selves and property.

It is nearly afternoon. A year ago we greeted hundreds who came to the funeral home and gathered at the church to honor Steve and comfort us. At home there were moments of laughter among the agonies of grief. I reread the memorial service: "I will not leave you comfortless. I will come to you." Comfort wore many faces this past year. Time filled in the depth of the wound, but has not healed it.

> *How have we cried?*
> *Let me count the ways:*
> *Body wracking sobs,*
> *Silent screams,*
> *Coursing tears,*
> *In anger,*
> *Through smiles,*
> *Long, short,*
> *Loud, soft,*
> *Often and less,*
> *For reasons there are,*
> *For those unknown,*
> *Repeating until*
> *We are void.*

22 May. This evening I recall our hardest trip, the return to Annapolis for Steve's burial.

"Often I think of the beautiful town
That is seated by the sea;
Often in thought go up and down
The pleasant streets of that dear old town. . .

"I remember the black wharves and the slips
And the sea tides tossing free . . .
And the beauty and mystery of the ships
And the magic of the sea . . .

"The drum-beat repeated o'er and o'er
And the bugle wild and shrill.
And the music of that old song
Throbs in my memory still . . .

"There are things of which I may not speak;
There are dreams that cannot die;
There are thoughts that make the strong heart weak,
And bring a pallor into the cheek,
And a mist before the eye.
And the words of that fatal song
Come over me like a chill:
'A boy's will is the wind's will,
And the thoughts of youth are long,
long thoughts. . . .'"   HENRY WADSWORTH LONGFELLOW

At 10:00 this morning I look at the clock (my great grandmother's) and this afternoon I heard its chimes again, like the bells from the campanile at Arlington. A year of collections and conversations in this notebook, my intimate. Few blank pages remain.

"Dear Mr. and Mrs. Lantz and Valeri,

My name is B—. I don't think we've met, but I am one of Steve's classmates from Eleventh Company. [She had been an usher at his Naval Academy memorial service.] The First Class in our company wanted you to know we have been thinking about Steve and your family the past few weeks. We felt he was with us throughout the busy events of Graduation Week. We would like you to know that we have placed flowers on Steve's grave in honor of our graduation."

The Second Mile

*"You would know the secret of death.
But how shall you find it unless
You seek it in the heart of life."* GIBRAN

The second year after Stephen's death. Healing continued, often with board and table games which long had been common family diversion—cribbage, backgammon or six-games-at-once marathons of *Kismet*, a game of fate. Another that we played was *Mille Bornes*, a thousand stones, the words referring to the cement kilometre-stones, or milestones that post road numbers and distances between European towns. As in this game, sometimes I progressed at average speed along the recovery route, sometimes ran out of gasoline.

At the bridge table last night, talk turned to the accomplishments and futures of our children. At times I must force myself to show interest in others. Despite having Valeri, I feel we were dealt a Coke hand.[H] We do little but contribute to the play this round, and feel we cannot take the lead. How long does the hand last?

Our good fortune used to frighten me. I confided to Mel,

"We are too lucky. We never have had serious problems like many of our friends, but that scares me when I wonder why. And I'm not trying to borrow trouble, either." Now we have a problem none of our friends have: we are the first to have a child die. We are a minority. It's not comfortable being a minority. And now we must continue to lean on that previous good fortune, maybe for a long time.

After Stephen died, someone commented, "I know this may not be much consolation, but at least you were blessed with a son that I shall never have." Ah, yes, the perfect family, a son and a daughter. Content to be an ordinary family, now when I hear that cancer strikes one in four, I want to bawl, "I wish to Heaven we weren't so damned average." Shall I pity parents who never had children like ours? Pity those who had them but cast aside appreciation for them? Pity others who wanted children but could not be parents? No, rationalizing is a phantom consoler, and being greedy, I continue to pity myself. In the Family Circus cartoon tonight one brother asks another who is crying, "Aren't your eyes empty yet?"

Whenever something would go awry for us on the thirteenth of any month, we would say, "Friday the 13th came on a Tuesday, or whichever day, this month."

Friday the thirteenth really came on Friday this month, the thirteenth since Steve's death. Such a long cruise. More than a year ago the date fell on Sunday. Will that number always trip a steady heartbeat?

The mourning doves do not chorus as long nor as plaintively as last year. Even the plants seem to have more vigor. And Mel and I are persistent in working toward a better relationship. Perhaps we know we must if marriage and healing are to go on, together.

"Death is growth," I told B—. "If we don't keep growing we regress. And regression is depression is backsliding to grief." So, I try to keep growing, but sometimes straddle the fence.

Life is like a limbo, too. As we dance under the ever lowering bar, we must become more aware of doing our best until we squeeze under for the final pass.

Stephen had wanted to contribute financially to his sister's post-high school education, his only reason, "It's just something I want to do." After his death I remembered that conversation, so from his estate, Mel and I established a special account for Valeri. The first opportunity to use a portion of his gift arose when she discovered a summer drama program at Chautauqua Institution in New York. I urged enrollment to further her vocational exploration, perhaps heal better away from home and not have to endure another summer of missing him. Selfishly, I needed conditioning for the day when she, too, would leave for college.

How often I have remarked that the real reason for parents is to rear children to become independent, productive persons living away from home. "Don't you miss him terribly?" friends asked when Steve went to the Academy. "Not really. He's where he should be, fulfilling a dream." When he left us at the motel on I-day (Induction), I was so happy, albeit sad. Goodbyes are that—semi-glad, semi-sad. The glad part is lost when one must let go forever. I shall miss Valeri more than I missed Steve; yet maybe because of his being gone, I shall miss her more. But when she leaves, I want to be able to answer as before; and I can begin with Chautauqua. Already, I anticipate letters about new faces and places, successes and, yes, disappointments, too.

For a couple of years, Valeri's and my relationship had been edgy. Under normal circumstances, mothers and teenage daughters may be estranged; but our rift was widened by grief. Complaining to E— about one tense situation, she sagely reminded, "I realize how difficult it is for you because you have lost your only son, but Val has lost her only brother." So together

Valeri and I drove to Chautauqua. The four-day mini-holiday presented an environment for our dialogue to begin, while the following six weeks gave each time and new space to build understanding unencumbered by day to day aggravations and physical closeness.

Driving past the Cleveland airport exit this morning as I returned from Chautauqua, my thoughts flew. I remembered Steve's many transfers there, Pat's fatal flight over a far-off airfield, Valeri's and my trip to Pat's funeral and our stopover there. Why are so many of our treasures buried beneath the earth, or under dark and heavy thoughts?

At lunch time I called home to give Mel my ETA (estimated time of arrival) and was shocked to hear of the auto accident which killed a friend. As I ate, I tried once more to put the pieces together! At the moment of death, the spirit rents the bonds of flesh, soars above the plains, the clouds, the planes, streaks toward light, knows beginning.

Why does Death peering over my shoulder inspire me to write? To the dying: you are leaving us, but you do not leave us disinherited. You leave the legacy of your years, your soul, your talents. The world changed when you arrived; it will change when you leave. We leave you—not on a rugged precipice, but on the brink of life. Carry what we gave for your journey; know that you left more for the remainder of ours; and we thank you for being you.

Uninvited, sadness came to sit on the porch tonight. Now there are two to miss. We expected a letter from Valeri. It did not come. Maybe tomorrow. How I wish Stephen could have been here for supper. No pesky flies, now that the patio is enclosed. I hope there are no insects to mar his hereafter!

With a portion of Stephen's bequest we purchased outdoor eating comfort. We spelled relief, from insects, s-c-r-e-e-n-s. How hateful flies and mosquitos were to him. Whether hiking in the woods or paddling a canoe, his head would be ringed with a halo of gnats or worse pesters, his charismatic chemistry tempting them as the Siren tinkling of the Good Humor truck woos a child. Like a pilot Ace scoring his hits, Steve exuberantly wielded a swatter against any winged invaders of a patio barbeque. "Why do you think I chose the Navy?" he questioned. "Didja ever see these rotten pests at sea?"

Parents search for runaways. Young street-people sleep in doorways, join sects, turn to strangers in community-sponsored shelters for counseling, referrals, bed and board. What severed their family bonds, alienated those who most need each other?

We mourn if our children loved us and are gone. We cry when they have hated us and left. We despair if our children ignore, misunderstand us. It hurts to remember the union of parent and child, no longer feel closeness. Why cannot it be? Who keeps it from us? you? me?

Home again from Chautauqua with Val. Another year older. R— came, as did E—, then Paula and the other C—'s (her family) and Mother and Dad. All joined to make my birthday happy. Despite all their efforts, tonight I could cry as Val did, all the way home. Hard goodbyes. At times during the day I felt Stephen near, but never near enough. Another year on which I can see his face only in a photograph.

We saw Stephen there, near Chautauqua, peering over boulders while we hiked at Panama Rocks, like he had spied from stony outcroppings along other trails. Chugging around the lake on the steamboat, I saw him peering into the engine room of another sternwheeler that once ferried us across the Mississippi. He's with us at landmarks, too; but we can't hear his monologues that used to accompany our inquests into history. We rarely needed guidebooks then. And I see him in the sampler I'm working for Bart and Charla's wedding at the Naval Academy. How I wish it were for Steve and Paula. They had planned an August wedding too, here, so grandparents would not have so far to travel.

Last year I saw him through walls of tears; now more often it is with but one tear in the corner of an eye, a furtive swallow, or maybe even a grin. Of all I've written, this seems the least self-pitying; but I shall read it tomorrow and decide.

What Is a Son?

He is the rush of a proud father's words,
"I got my boy!"
And a mother's quiet joy with
her first born, a son.
Smiling brown eyes
peering through
peek-a-boo fingers or
hanging over rocks to
ambush your heart as you pass;
an open mouth
to fill with chocolate anything,
an open mind
to fill with tales of war and yore,
and always more;
an open heart and open arms
to cradle the sad or pained.
Smitten with life,
he is a strong, tanned hand
clutching a blue blanket,
a pink bunny,
a puppy leash or
the flag held high.
He is ideals and inspiration,
a giver and a gift,
God's promise of a better man.

Early morning and I sit in conflictive contemplation. My third trip to the Chapel. This time I feel we are Steve's proxies. The sampler is ready. I review the prayer I was asked to write for the reception, and pray for myself in a second, close breath.

Father, Look well upon these new wearers of wedding bands, symbols of Your holy and ordained way for man and woman to live. Let their rings be unbroken circles of love, like ring binders on a new chapter in their books of life, as bonds of trust and mutual and equal responsibility in marriage, symbols for Your encircling arms. Walk with them in times of disagreement, hardship, separation, sorrow or despair. Let them not know many of these times; but when they come, let them depend upon Your swift help. Let them remember to thank You for also walking with them in times of agreement, prosperity, togetherness, joy and hope; and let them know many of these. Let them grow in love and life, never forgetting their best Teacher; and let that be the prayer of all, both here and in our thoughts. . . .

I am unsure of myself; I have never tried to write for others. The pen I'm using came from the hospital. Its imprint says, What we are is God's gift to us. What we become is our gift to God. What am I yet to become because of Stephen? Gibran wrote that the significance of a man is not what he attains, but rather what he longs to attain. Once again I am unsure — of my longings.

I have yet to finish healing. In dark passageways of time and images I grope. Fingers of light fringe closed doors. When they open, laughter spills over their threshholds. All the beautiful people are inside — Zest [for life], Hope, Faith, Love, Peace [of Mind]. They beckon me to enter. I stand outside and cry because I do not feel like mingling. Sometimes I think I shall never achieve inner peace again except in my own death.

I am reading a book about healing physical illness from within. My grief, too, must be healed from within my mind. Tears, ink, reminiscences — strange salves and Bandaids for a sorrowing soul.

Paying scant attention to its résumé, but intrigued by its title, I mail-ordered the book Healing from Within. The headway toward recovery that I had made with physical activity was furthered when I transposed the author's concepts of health management (intended for those with somatic illness) into personalized applications and exercises in self-communication and constructive behavior.

- Riveting on the cause of my grief enabled me to purge it with tears, a previously unacceptable solution to problems. "How are you doing?" people ask.
  "I have shed fifty years of tears."
- If an activity bred depression, I stopped it, undertook another or countered the feeling: When did I last feel good about this situation? And then I fixed on details from that experience.
- When emotional strain built, I took an interval to stretch and deep breathe. Thoughts could be uncluttered by limiting them to a single concentration: the churning within a cloud, waves and sand jumbling at the water's edge, the moil of an anthill, images or associations provoked by a line of poetry or prose.
- I enumerated the positive aspects of my life, or projected what it might become in ten years if an imagined opportunity presented itself. Daydreaming, a formerly uncommon pastime, surprisingly uplifted me.
- Normally annoyed by excessive sound, I now sporadically immersed myself in the double forte volume from a favorite recording.
- When time or distance prevented travel, my mind and I eloped to tranquility amid sand dunes or leaf-layered glades.[11]

Today I cleaned and sorted driftwood. Steve would have liked many pieces we've collected recently. Some may have been from his last trips to Lake Michigan with Paula. He brought me wildflowers from the field that summer, too, like when he was a little boy, and shells and coral from his cruise in the Caribbean. How he wanted the Mediterranean assignment! "You'll have plenty of other opportunities to go there," I had said when we would talk of my trip to Majorca. I had bought a chess set there for his collection. Checkmate.

I do not write about the best part of my days yet. Perhaps I should. Even if Stephen's book is closed, he continues to write parts of mine. But I am still afraid of hurts which can rip my pages; and sometimes I wonder how many chapters are left?

We saw Bart and Charla married at the Academy, but first went to the florist and then to Arlington. As I knelt arranging the flowers, I began to feel despondent. But then a voice seemed to whisper, Do not stand by my grave and weep. I am not here. I do not sleep. I am a thousand winds that blow. . . . I heard no more, remembered no more of the poem sent to me a year ago; but I felt no more sadness. It was enough to carry me through the ensuing days. Mel, however, was sadder back East. "Steve seemed so close," he said; and I am sorry that feeling does not comfort him as it does me.

"You cannot say, you must not say
That he is dead. He is just away!
With a cheery smile and a wave of the hand
He has wandered into an unknown land
And left us dreaming how very fair
It needs must be since he lingers there;
So think of him faring on, as dear
in the love of There as the love of Here
Think of him still the same, and say,
He is not dead, he is just away." JAMES WHITCOMB RILEY

I called Pat's mother (in Texas) on this anniversary of his death. Afterward I felt how unreal it was for me to be speaking with her, only because of our common reason to know each other. The same disbelief came as I sat at Arlington. How can this be me? C'est vrai. Je suis ici. C'est moi. Verdad. Estoy aqui. Soy yo. I know no other ways to say what is real. Still, a long nightmare from which I may yet awaken?

Hanging on the bathroom wall, my crewel field of grasses swarms with shell butterflies, reminds me of our trip to Ocracoke. On hands and knees we four finger-sifted white sands in search of tiny purple and yellow coquinas for my intended stitchery. And Steve ran the shoreline to tone up for the months ahead in Plebe training. "The last long vacation we shall be able to take together, maybe for a long time," I had said before we left. And it was. Kübler-Ross spoke of butterflies signifying life. Like butterflies, my thoughts flit over the sands of yesterdays.

The *goodliest land under the cope of heav'n* the Raleigh colonists praised the North Carolina coast. *Winds carry whispers of shipwrecked souls and echoes of whinnying wild ponies. Once peopled with noblemen and maverick pioneers, runaway slaves and old salts, some beaches today are rife with vacationers and too many of their accouterments; but we sought more remote stretches of sand broadcast with the nautical debris from old merchants or marauders, dotted with skeletons of sea creatures, guarded by lighthouse sentinels stately dressed in black and white, patrolled by pelican and willet. A* goodliest *holiday for us.*

*How we yearn to touch the past! We browsed an antique show today where dealers offer pieces of history for sale, ofttimes trôp chères [*too expensive*]. We admired the craftsmanship and bought another bit of yesterday. Sometimes we spend extravagantly to own another family's treasure. Oh, the nostalgia of our family heirlooms and our own ancestors framed on the walls! How we yearn to touch the past. We browse memory to retrieve moments, but there is no price we would not pay to own again some of those instants.*

En route one summer day to their grandmother's house up the street, Stephen dumped his thirteen-month-old sister head-over-stroller-tray into the sand as they raced across a field with other young friends and their baby brother. However, he neglected to divulge the incident until one lunch hour more than three years later. While he never lied or hid much from us, he was astute in shielding his parents from an occasional situation until they were capable of rational response.

"Was Valeri hurt?"

"Nah, just a faceful of sand, but it was pretty soft. She was more shook up than anything."

"Did she cry?"

"Yeah, she yelled a lot; but there wasn't any blood, so I didn't think she was hurt bad. The sand brushed right off her bonnet and coat, and we got her cleaned up good before we got to Maw-Maw's."

"How did you clean her face?" How readily children learn expediency from their parents!

"Spit."

My grandfather made wine from a small planting of grapes in the hollow behind his house. During one visit, Mel's interest was piqued; and fermentation soon came to fruition at our home in an early attempt with dandelions.

Stephen and Valeri were drafted to collect blossoms from the most luxuriant plants they could locate, which, to their relief, grew on the neighborhood school grounds and not in someone's yard. Nonetheless, they groused with good humor, "Everyone else gets rid of dandelions. Not us. We gotta scrounge buckets of the best. Nah, we're not crazy; we're just different."

Soon afterward the basement reeked, as is normal, with the second step in Mel's winemaking experiment. Worse, the odor found permanent, bottled lodging. Wines should have bouquet; but even after years of aging, this dandelion unpotable was still fusty! Subsequently, Mel produced wine from several fruits and cultivated his own vines which now yield a substantial second crop, our grapevine wreaths!

Like new wines, some lives are finished (perfected) and bottled early. Others need to age, to improve. Some will go acid or die; the wines cannot know what they will be.

> "Let fate do her worst; there are relics of joy
> Bright dreams of the past which she cannot destroy;
> Which come in the night-time of sorrow and care,
> And bring back the features that joy used to wear.
> Long, long be my heart with such memories fill'd!
> You may break, you may shatter this vase, if you will,
> But the scent of the roses will hang 'round it still."
> THOMAS MOORE

I do not want fall to come so soon again. I am not ready for the sleeping, the dormancy, the dying that it summons; and melancholia strums my melodium.

For some, classes and projects, new or renewed relationships spell Beginning; but my mind repeats The End and I must wait longtemps *for Spring. It is good to rest; so must we all. But some will lie down never to rise again, like a monarch's haphazard flutterings that preface its fatal pause.*

Flamboyant-hued leaves flitter and whirligig earthward. Squirrels secret a winter hoard and man mimics in cellar, jar and freezer. Leafsmoke drifts like fragrant fog. The performance is well-rehearsed, Nature Presents! But I lament the closing of the show.

Choruses of ducks and geese cross to exit, cajole in symphonies of flight and sound. Their gabble never fails to draw me to the window, those robust farewells from V's of honkers winging south. Vainglorious vagabonds, their flight pattern is their monogram. Nature is fraught with compulsion in autumn—migrating, storing, retooling for the advancing season—but my nature has long decried the harbingers.

As an alternative to holidays of sightseeing or camping, we purchased timesharing at a near-home resort. Tucked between the pages of a book forgotten by a previous occupant of our vacation apartment, the title of the yellowed clipping restated my seething.

Hold Fast the Summer
"It is the beauty of the day and all it contains—
The laughter and work and finally the sleep.
The quiet—
Oh, September, do not put your weight upon my mind.
For I know he will be going,
This son of mine who is now a man—he must go.
Time will lace my thoughts with joyous years.
The walls will echo his "Hello."
His caring will be around each corner.
His tears will be tucked into our memory book.
Life calls him beyond our reach—to different walls,
New faces, shiny halls, shy smiles, many places.
Greater learning—he must go. But wait, before he leaves,
Be sure he knows you love him.
Hide the lump in your throat as you hug him.
He'll soon be home again—but he will be different.
The little boy will have disappeared.
How I wish I could take September and shake it,
For it came too soon.
I must look to the beauty of each new day
And silently give thanks." AUTHOR UNKNOWN

The initial trial of the new vacation experience left us anticipating future weeks. Perhaps Mel and I needed the time alone more that year than we would need it in the future; but a specific side benefit for me was diminished fall doldrums, a renewed effort to look outward.

At the beach, white caps porpoise on the shore like lemmings rushing in reverse, dash themselves on golden sand. Mallards groove to rock 'n roll, croak a raucous laugh-quack to unseen comedians inside. Feathered scavengers scuttle. Juveniles foil pecking orders, snatch strewings when the aged are sated. Gulls screech and plunge for tidbits tossed aloft in sport by apterous adults, while black masked swans, aloof in ermine finery, scorn the fracas.

Home again. I need more investments, new sources of strength. My inner resources seem depleted again, and I don't know where to turn. There's God, of course; but I need verbal intercourse, feedback from a human; yet I don't want to overdraw friends' time. I have resumed volunteering at The Civic [theater] and the hospital. More irony. I, who now have so little confidence in planning far ahead, am elected chair of long-range planning for the church. Even these groups do not suffice. Frantically we pursue the tangible, the here and now, the hear and react. Wondering, I still wander through some days. "It is only by risking our persons from one hour to another that we live at all." (William James) Perhaps I do not risk often enough. Risk was a favorite war game of Stephen's.

We received a letter from T— today. Dear T—. He gave Steve his D and B trousers when Stephen's couldn't be found for burial. T— is shipboard now. His letter was dated 13 October. Was he as aware of that number as I?

Three pairs of Steve's shoulder boards (rank insignia) perch on the door casing of his room. An unfinished ship model sits on a shelf; one or two await repairs. His friends smile at me from pictures. Still undisturbed, Steve's room comforts me. We often talk about him as if he were only away; yet in the depths I know he is never coming back to his room again.

At fifteen, Stephen wanted to repaint his room. "Fine," I agreed, "What did you have in mind?"

"Well, I'm thinking about camouflage." Silence. "You know, something like super graphics on the walls."

"All the walls?"

"Yeah, what do you think?"

Combat chromatics? "I think saying, 'It would be different' might be a gross understatement, but let me think about it."

I looked around. Along one wall were tanks, ships and planes, models aligned and moored on floor to ceiling shelf-fields. Overhead, tiny World War I pilots engaged in dogfights; the Blue Angels streaked out from their corner; and Axis fuselages trailed cotton wisps as they plunged to defeat from the Allied barrages, all suspended from monofilament lines that criss-crossed beneath rockets and spacecraft painted on the ceiling light fixture.

With no more hesitation and little reservation I vouched, "I think it would be great! Two conditions, though: I want to help choose colors so it doesn't simulate some murky jungle encampment; and you must repaint it when you tire of it, or leave home for good."

Elated, Steve selected colors, sketched gigantic free-form designs and created a unique bivouac. I always intended to purchase material from military surplus to sew curtains, but my stimulus died when he left for college.

> *The camouflage is gone. Yesterday Stephen's walls were repainted, blotted out. Today I finished the trim and am depressed. A year and a half. Was it too soon?*
>
> *I thought I was ready. If Mel or Val had a contrary opinion, neither expressed it when I first proposed redecorating. So, the decision was mine; but now I rue the choice. Well, it's only the walls. Stephen is not painted out, erased from mind or life. I hope he likes it now, blue like before.*

Newly furnished with a sofabed for guests and an antique oak secretary that earlier I had refinished, alterations in Stephen's bedroom neared completion. But the closet and chest, bookcase and walls continued to teem with his memorabilia; their displacement would not be dictated by death. *Steve's room became my office-retreat.*

> *"Each one must find a quiet place*
> *Within his heart where he may go*
> *To find himself, and for a space*
> *Drink deeply where still waters flow."* INGA CALDWELL

> *As I sit here in Stephen's room and write letters, musings or mundanes in checkbooks and ledgers, I am aware of his absence, his presence. As time slips away, Stephen seems to, too; and it is painful to realize how far he really is from my world. Somewhere I have read of an Eastern philosophy which suggests that the soul will reside near earth as long as anyone remembers the person. And believers live to serve unselfishly with kind words and good works so when they die, their souls will remain in the afterlife of memory. I am uncertain of this*

precept, but I do feel Steve's presence that sometimes seems stronger than mere memory. It is difficult to explain and many would scoff; but I just whisper, "Hello, Love."

Life is not Solitaire; we are self-insufficient in providing for physical needs, in meeting emotional demands. From ancient times and diverse cultures people have looked to a Power, be he/she called Allah, Buddha, Christ, Confucius, God, Jehovah, Mohammed or any other Name to which they turn when mortal power is limited. [After one setback in the ICU] I urged Steve to say, "I have carried this burden so long. Please, Lord, take it for awhile to rest me so that I can gain strength to carry it again."

And now it is time for me to carry more, to put my accounts in order. How much do I owe for what I am, and to whom? Can I ever repay them or even cancel the debt? Not knowing my timetable, dare I defer payment until a more convenient time? How shall I choose among those with needs, to invest my time and contributions, and how much shall I give to them and to my own deficits? The ordering of those debit-credit columns is far more complex than those that I do for the IRS!

I have tried to balance other accounts (activities) this fall. Crafts occupy more hours, but I do not persevere to complete them without a gift-deadline; and it doesn't seem to matter that projects for our use plateau, partially concluded. Maybe other parts of my life follow this pattern too; but at least in both I make beginnings again. I still need to write, but fewer of my thoughts center on death.

> *Sunset clouds*
> *like gossamer stoles,*
> *iridescent gold and*
> *crimson slashed, mauve sashed*
> *gowns of sky sylphs*
> *trailing silver twilight capes.*

Because distance separated Mel's family from ours, his sister's invitation to an Army-Notre Dame football game at South Bend promised a pleasant fall outing; but as the weekend approached, my apprehension surfaced.

I do not anticipate the trip to South Bend to see a group of young men in uniforms. Our trip three years ago when Navy played there is still too well-remembered.

Steve looked so tired from his school schedule and the all-night bus ride. Since D and B weren't marching, I told him he should have cancelled; but he didn't want to disappoint any of us. Navy's loss was the only imperfection of that day. We told him his graduation gift had been ordered. "Wow! Already? I guess now I'll have to graduate." "You will." "Yeah, I'm sure I will. I just hope I never disappoint you." "You never will." He never did. And Mom has not finished her graduation gift for him, a quilt of naval history in embroidered ships. So much for long-range planning.

Despite Stephen's enthusiasm for the military, he knew the futility of war. Yet, he saw himself as a champion of right, and visible force as a deterrent to invasion. As an impressionable youth, I had been appalled by the slaughters of combat in World War II and its concentration camps, by Hiroshima and Nagasaki, by the Korean conflict. Had I been draftable, I was always uncertain of my course. He and I disagreed about escalating preparedness. "I don't understand how you can be so supportive of me and my commitment when you seem to be so opposed to the military," he would argue.

"I am opposed to war as a means to peace, to the insanity of overkill, to the annihilation that modern war implies. Still, each must follow one's own conscience, and I respect and am proud of the fervor you have for your principles and duty. Most of us are too apathetic about everything. And I am also aware that were it not for people like you, perhaps people like me would not be able to enjoy our idealism!"

"Not till a treachery is proved
His sword the patriot soldier draws;
War is the last alternative—
Be patient till you know the cause.
Meanwhile—Half-mast o'er all the land
The verdict wait; your wrath restrain;
Half-mast! for all the gallant band—
The martyrs of the Maine." [1] LLOYD MIFFLIN [12]

    Christmas is sadness still. The season holds lackluster appeal. Christmas is writing notes again to our friends and to Steve's whom I would not be writing were he here. My German Santa (doll) has a pensive face. Like me, he was from the Depression era. Perhaps his face reflects that period, my present stupor. Santa's spirit: ill-promoted in our economy, overinflated by our merchandising, distorted by us. Santa lives at the North Pole, visits shopping malls, rings bells on street corners, sees his likeness on paper and plastic everything. For brief weeks he is a northern Brigadoonian who cannot even tarry for the New Year, who is upstaged by two babes who also rout old Father Time. Too soon we retire the Christmas spirit. Yet, new does replace old, and with the celebration of each new year we grasp for hope and resolution in life.

    Home for Christmas, three of Stephen's friends came to visit tonight. Talking about their futures counteracted my dejection, for their enthusiasm is contagious. The planter they brought will remind me of them, and its growth will parallel theirs in separate ventures far from here, after their graduations.

    January again. The icy fingers of its days caress me like death described in books. Memory icicles pierce the concentration of my mind, or melting, drum a somber Musak background. Another year joylessly begun. Sitting by the fire, *rapt in a symphony, I can absorb warmth and am soothed: Blustering cold freezes reveries, dispirits. Flick'ring flames thaw chilled fingers, toes and thoughts. Headlong arpeggios and crescendos drown apprehension, and scuffling thoughts are dispersed by stringed sonatas.*

The bleakness of that notation was dispelled further at the community theater where again I could escape in rehearsals for a play, *The Eccentricities of a Nightingale*, by Tennessee Williams.

Acting brings a magic to my life—allows me to explore the minds of persons I could never know, to understand more fully the ones I do. The deranged mother from Williams' imagination has challenged me, made real the reality of madness.

At rehearsal tonight I lost contact with the actions around me, being immersed in the figments of my character's world of escape. I returned to the set with a jolt and knew I had missed cues. It was sobering to realize how simple it can be to slip away from the hurtful eccentricities of life, to divorce oneself from painful scenes, fraternize with kinder faces of fantasy become real. And so anyone faced with death or a tortured life may decide to cross up center, peel off the mortal masque and exit to the backstage of the mind.

Where have all the good men gone? *(was the Valentine grumble of a young woman writing in a local news magazine).* Well, I have one of them. I remember former loves, but know I would not be happier than with the one I chose twenty-four years ago. The good man (or woman) is more unselfish than self-centered, concerned more than fifty percent of the time with his partner's welfare over his own. If fortunate, each partner will give and receive that greater-than-half share, and this overlap bonds the union.

Stephen and Valeri could not have been without our pairing. We need to tell each other of love and caring, again and often. One may not always dine on gourmet love, but an occasional helping of leftovers will not harm the diner. And passion must sometimes be prefixed with c-o-m.

Yet, death complicates; for when someone dies, we don't know what to do with the leftover love. We cannot serve it to another because feelings for each are singular. So we must savor each morsel of time spent with one we love; for when all time is devoured, the memory of the morsel will be too heavily seasoned with salt the second time around.

"Hours fly
Flowers die.
New days,
New ways
Pass by,
Love stays."   HENRY VAN DYKE

March 30, after the shooting of the President. When I first heard the news from E—'s phone call, I was scarcely moved. The deed is terrible; yet we hear or read so often of similar acts of violence that one of us has done to another. Then I mulled over my lack of response. Are assassination and murder so commonplace in my world that I fail to react with outrage? Do emotional calluses grow like a cancer without remission or a cure? Has society numbed us to suffering, injustice and killing to the extent that we are neither unduly surprised nor shocked at the news of more? Do others feel the same apathy? Do they admit it? Where next do our feelings lead about the value of life and the perpetrators of barbarism? We wonder if we suffer abominations to learn. Do we learn? Do we even wonder anymore?

Too short a life? Too sad a song? Too busy to care? Tch-tch, it's wrong: Too self-serving to be sensitized.

May. Despite the passage of time, the mind is loath to forget the fury of a tornado. Television weather "W's," watches and warnings, bayings from sirens activated in error or in rehearsal, the piercing whine of a windstorm, particularly after nightfall—all will alert one to evalute their immediate significance.

Storm!
Darkness.
Gales pommel the air
like the sound of a furious sea.
They demand our listening, shriek, soften,
fill ebony space with Wagnerian timbres
that coax our thoughts out there
to critique the thunderous concert.
Quiet retards the din.
An interval of rests, repeated,
hushes rampage, summons calm before
el fine.
Applause!

The anniversary of Stephen's death approaches discreetly, like a model undertaker who reminds by his presence. Two years. So long. So short. What have we done with all those days?

Shadows of mistakes loom. Wistfully we wonder if we're on the right path, the best road. Patience has not grown much. Is there patience in Stephen's world? There must be some ebbing of this chafing, for I cannot envision a hereafter filled with grieving relatives and impatient souls.

Valeri has shared much this year. She's bursting with news when she comes from school, like Stephen used to be, and we talk awhile before she or I need to be busy with homework or home work. Now I do not seem to be so much a burden or a threat to her or whatever, aside from death, caused the hiatus in our relationship. It's more solid, like the one I had with him; but it does not remind me of him, for I am immersed in her. I am grateful all over again for the family closeness we had, for what we still have. If she and I can continue to build, we'll have another year to grow before she leaves, and hopefully more all-nighters of our own whenever she comes home.

Many say, "I hate Goodbye's." Our common tragedies led M— (whose son met instantaneous death in a traffic fatality) to inquire of E—, our mutual friend, "Is her grief different from mine? At least she was with him, had time to say goodbye. Does that help?"

"I don't think there's much difference in your grief," E— replied. "After the shock that each of you has known, the loss you feel seems to be the same."

Yet one day long after her brother died, Valeri would comment, "If Brother had to die, at least I'm glad we could be there, to say goodbye." A contraction of *God be with you,* like the French *Adieu.* I do not hate *goodbye's* but appreciate M—'s feeling of having been robbed, even of that most hurtful moment.

A couple I know always stand at their door to wave goodbye when anyone leaves. Why? To remember and be remembered in the event this farewell is final. Morbid? Not really, for while we do not want to live intimidated by death, we should take leave confident that no harsh word will later echo unforgiven, no small favor was shelved for a more convenient time, that the parting hug will continue to hold, the smile be carried forever.

> *The clock has just struck midnight signalling the beginning of that fateful day two years ago. None of us speaks of those chilling weeks in May, yet even as I strove to bring sunshine to Val's birthday, thoughts intruded with the clouds of Stephen's last day. Today we'll hang the flag again.*

> *The beginning of the third year since we left Stephen's body at Arlington. The words* You'll Never Walk Alone *leaped at me from rows of graduation greetings on the card rack today, and I chose that one for a midshipman friend. I have yet to always keep up front the message that I do not walk alone. The hurt is better but lingers despite anything I say or do. And I must turn again to faith; for there is no answer to why Steve died, only more answers now to why I'm living. Maybe as he wanted to make his little sister laugh, I can make a sister or brother laugh—or at least cry with them when she or he stumbles on a boulder in the road.*

The second mile.
A stone marks two among
mille bornes,
a thousand stones
that mark the years
along the way.

The second mile.
A life, one gift among
mille dons,
a thousand gifts;
no lurking thief
to steal the lot.

The second mile.
A melody among
mille chants,
a thousand airs
and hours long
to sing the song
of Stephen. 13 May.

June. Unexpectedly, I am stricken with grief but do not know why. It has been a long time since I have felt its weight so heavily. I have a second premonition of death like the one which left me coldly awake one night last week when I dreamed of D—'s dying. In my dream we had to hurry to say things left unsaid for too long, for this time there was no time left. The scimitar of death hangs ever o'er our necks.

A few days later, Mel telephoned from work with news that shocked: a colleague's son and childhood friend of Stephen had been killed in an automobile accident. Born in January, both boys celebrated pre-school birthday parties, fantasized backyard exploits, *slept-over* in like pairs of clown-striped pajamas that Mel's mother had made for Stephen. Giggling long after *lights out,* they plotted adventures for tomorrow.

Stephen's pal has joined him. Neither had enough tomorrows. After Mel's call, I found snapshots of them in their bright p.j.'s. Mel called them mites.

Two Mites.
"Say Brett, what's out there to explore?"
"A world of space and heroes, games of war,
ice cream cones 'n chocolate, and more."
"Say, Steve, what more is to explore?"
"Gee, I don't know, we've just begun; but
bikes, new friends, Scouts and school will come,
swimming, fishing, ball games, wishing or
just some time to run.
It's all out there, my friend,
great stuff for you and me;
but while we're waiting, guy,
Let's go climb a tree!"

Stephen's old Scout troop published a paper drive ad to raise funds for camping equipment. I wonder what vehicle has replaced their sometimes-dependable old school bus. A different scoutmaster came with one of the boys who smiled shyly when I answered the door and never spoke a word during many trips up and down the basement stairs. "Good job," the leader said as they worked together. I am reminded of our years with Scouts and Brownies and of adventures with the umbrella tent we no longer use which I also gave them. As they left I smiled, another chapter wrapped up. No nostalgia.

Labor Day weekend. Mel sought added relief from the veterinarian for Boots, our greying old fellow of dubious ancestry who now was wracked with creeping spinal arthritis. The doctor's prognosis offered nothing but the fore-prescribed solution, an injection which would bring our pet permanent respite from pain.

Stephen is in my thoughts this week. Is it because of Boots? Has Steve been with us as we walk again with death? Fifteen years, another long segment of experiences to bury as we continue to gain even more experience in matters of dying than we want. Yet, the inevitability of death must not hang like widow's weeds to obscure our acceptance of it as a part of life.

Tagged *sea dew* by Pliny and exalted through the centuries, the legends of my favorite herb appeal to me as much as its culinary virtues. Carried in festivals and funerals, strewn in banquet halls and homes, it could *gladeth one, away evil spirits,* rekindle lost energy and heal. Tossed on a grave,

> *Rosemary is for immortality and friendship, for remembrance. ". . . there's rosemary, that's for remembrance; pray you love, remember. . . ." (Ophelia, Hamlet) Already I have a lifetime supply dried from the garden of my life.*
>
> *Anniversaries approach again, the third since Stephen died, [but first] rehearsals for another play, Christmas holidays and our wedding anniversary.*

So, love prevailed and Mel and I remained together. Why? Maybe tenacity is inherent in Scandinavian and Teutonic genes, or marriage vows were not to be regarded flippantly the first time *for worse* came to live with us. Perhaps we held fast to patience, gradually released self-absorption. Maybe we refused to panic in a bear market, sell out a good investment when the dividends appeared to plummet, remembered high past yields. Perhaps chemistry and all the other bonding that connected us in the beginning, strong in its beginning and tended afterward, kept the union from dissolving in an acid test. Maybe we wanted to try to be third generation golden year partners, like my parents and grandparents. And throughout, our Silent Partner never divorced us.

On his last Christmas, Steve gave Mel and me a nut dish, a gold-lined, silver scuttle. "I have no idea why I bought that," he commented as I opened the package. "At the time it seemed like a great choice, but I've never given you anything like that before. Now I think I should have shopped more."

"Not at all. We have nothing like it, and it's quite lovely. I know we shall enjoy it for many years."

How I shall miss Stephen this year, our silver year. Since he died we have continued to avoid much attention to the Season, but this year the family will not allow that; and I, too, feel incentive for more celebration. Valeri is planning and scurrying around, intent on making her open house (for our anniversary) a special evening for us. How I wish she had known an easier time of growing through the teens. "Fifteen going on fifty," I said to friends after her brother died. I can only hope those years will become a strong foundation for her understanding of life and love.

I still mourn for Steve's leaving so soon. In him we saw a bit of what each dreamed of being but were not, could not become, would never be. But we are better for having known and loved him, if only for awhile.

"And a woman who held a babe against her bosom said,
Speak to us of Children. And he said:
Your children are not your children.
They are the sons and daughters of
 Life's longing for itself.
They come through you but not from you, And though
 they are with you yet they belong not to you.
You may give them your love but not your thoughts,
For they have their own thoughts.
You may house their bodies but not their souls,
For their souls dwell in the house of tomorrow which
 you cannot visit, not even in your dreams.
You may strive to be like them, but
 seek not to make them like you,
For life goes not backward nor tarries with yesterday.
You are the bows from which
 your children as living arrows are sent forth. . . ."[13]

What shall I give this child of mine? How shall I protect him, without oversheltering? Who will he learn to respect? What are his legacies? What secrets that I know do I owe, which ones leave for him to discover?

You owe this child the lessons of life: Faith to endure, endurance to hope, hope to achieve, achievement for good and Love to underpin. Daily teach this child of yours, and Mine.

Eventually my mind was gutted of grief spilled into notebooks. In one of them is a quotation from Gandhi. "There is more to life than increasing its speed." One could substitute *bereavement recovery* for the word *life,* since each of us reaches that destination at his own pace, too.

Yet, there is danger in dawdling too long with loss, blaming bad luck, wasting one's days and talents. Like any overindulgence, mourning can become addictive. Prolonged despair desensitizes, damages mental health. One may be deluded that there is no harm to others; after all, grief is private. If this were true, however, support groups for families of the troubled would be unnecessary.

As in games, the grief-stricken can develop strategies to regain peace of mind, self-fulfillment and healthy relationships. Although a positive attitude (tomorrow will be better) will speed the progress, there is no jet transportation for the journey. Often the way appears impassable, the detours defeating, the milestones like millstones, the station too far, the fuel supply low. Those who have covered the route may help others map theirs, safely pick up a hitchhiker, be a Samaritan to the stranded.

Faith charted my course; Hope refueled me; Love was my transport to Healed. The greatest of these was Love. And as long as I glanced away frequently to break the hypnosis of that shadowed road, I kept providing answers to the question, What do I do with the rest of my life?

Standing on the shore of a placid pool, we toss in a pebble, soon lost to view. But impressions from its impact ripple outward in rings; and if we drop more pebbles, the circles interact until the whole surface of the pond is set alive. Grief may check the throwing hand, return the water to a mirror. But when the reflection of our own morose face engulfs us like some pining Narcissus, we may become enough repelled by that vision to start pitching stones again.

Half a century of life, a quarter of marriage. Many years, some tears, heaviness and lightness. Their blessings still outweigh despairs even when a golden pond hides uncharted holes to unsettle a wader.

As Ethel, (from On Golden Pond) *my words exhort my daughter Chelsea to come to terms with the past.* "Life marches by . . . I suggest you get on with it."[14] Emerson said it, too. "The days come and go, but they say nothing. And if we do not use the gifts they bring, they carry them as silently away."

Life is still like a book, my travel log. I began to add chapters again when I could re-match my stride with Life as strongly as I had with Death.

Postscripts

*"We will grieve not, rather find
Strength in what remains behind."*
WORDSWORTH

Serendipity! Like some self-cached combatant who hadn't heard of the armistice, a twenty-five-year-old tiny, plastic person shouldering a bazooka just emerged from the shrubbery and myrtle-festooned fieldstones in the small patio near our front door. The weather-worn GI, forest green on one side faded to slate blue on the other, now points his weapon at a bookcase item in *Steve's room*. Vines and time entwine objects and memories. They surprise but no longer wound us when they surface after we are healed and at peace.

Computers keep spewing address labels. Because I had neglected to remove Stephen's name from voter registration, book clubs and retail mailing lists, correspondence continues to arrive for him. I never could scrawl *Deceased* across an envelope and return it to the sender. Yet, because I did not, form letters still surface: *We've missed you. Surely you did not intend to let your subscription lapse.* Perhaps I keep hoping that *Due to rising postal costs, this catalogue is absolutely the last we can send without your new order.* Eight years afterward, communications to him persist while I patiently await their demise!

Although healing proceeded dissimilarly in each, we live with composure, much as before Steve died. More self-contained than mine, Mel's anguish was aired in thoughts borne on the winds that swayed the field grasses where he had walked alone or with Boots. He met death as he faces life, steadily and with measured progress. Valeri is pursuing a drama career in The Big Apple. Like her brother, she has a mature intensity of purpose and direction. Perhaps because of him, people, and especially her peers, recognize and benefit from her compassionate comprehension of their problems.

The *aloneness* I felt because our son died waned as awareness grew: I was not different from others who hurt; only circumstances were unique to each of us. Sometimes I am more patient now; often I am intolerant—of petty grievances and disregard for others. Distress caused indifference toward my own physical health; recovery restored responibility for holistic well-being. No longer perturbed by its tenuity, I plan for the future and avail myself of activities involving learning and expression through writing, theater, community access TV production and music. Mel and I set aside practice time for our new recorders. Although I did not resume piano lessons, I recaptured the joy of playing. Through study and service in the Stephen Ministries,[1] I grow in care-giving.

Three of Stephen's grandparents have died. My widowed eighty-year-old father did not allow visual impairment to deter his weekly visits to a nursing home where he brought to more than a dozen new friends a receptive ear from outside and bananas, rich in potassium, to combat their aches! Together they buffered loneliness, revived the old days, found incidents to laugh about, sang a ditty and, on rare occasions, carefully executed a brief two-step!

A photograph of our godson has its niche in the living room bookcase, near his namesake. Young Stephen was born to Charla and Bart who, as he wrote, have made us a part of their lives; and a niece and another best friend of Steve's have further bonded our families by also naming their first sons after ours.

We have returned to the Naval Academy on numerous occasions, once for the double wedding of Paula and her sister to midshipmen; and we have added snapshots of Paula and her beautiful children to an expanding gallery of *sons and daughters* on the walls of *Steve's room.*

After the local memorial service, a pallbearer hugged me. "I just hope you can use lots more sons, Mrs. Lantz." Not long ago he dropped in to chat about his *new* life, 1400 miles away. Before leaving he said, "I always plan to keep in touch. You're very special to me, like Steve was." And so Navy and civilian friends continue to touch our lives with phone calls, wedding and birth announcements, photos and scenic cards that sometimes bear, in the upper right hand corner, the face of a foreign dignitary!

Sorrow isn't forever, love is.

Steve's outlook on life first spurred a junior high friendship that *bottomed out* during high school with their conflicting politics and ideals, but which was reestablished later as each moderated toward the middle. Scott wrote,

"When Steve died, I was a little lonelier and a lot older. I missed his enthusiasm for everything he did, wondered how to develop that quality so that I could accomplish something with my life before they were burying me.

"When I thought about Steve's [critical] words in my yearbook, now coming to me out of his grave to haunt me, push me, I realized that love, not spite motivated them. Just getting by would never bring me happiness. I needed a cause for which my conscience would not allow a poor attitude.

"Working with farmers in the village as a Peace Corps volunteer made me feel needed. My hard work brought tangible results; I was helping people live better. I had found

something that would have made Steve proud to have been my friend.

"I'm in graduate school now, learning how to improve international aid programs. I'm near the top of my class because when my energy flags, I remember one of two things: either Steve's time capsule to me, or the distended stomachs of the children of my friends in Zaire. Then my strength returns."

The marks of a person: what one longs to be, what one leaves behind. Long after the ship is lost to sight, its wake is visible to remind us of the course that was set.

At Bethesda Hospital I learned that emotion can cloud the reasoning that would direct one's hand to disconnect life support systems. Given a similarly hopeless situation with a family member, I believe I now could act rather than react. If he or she is resolute, who am I to refuse them the exchange of existence under total machination for life!

Abraham Lincoln said, "Sorrow comes with bitterest agony." It did. He also promised, "You are sure to be happy again." We are. A friend wrote that we would "need time to surrender the past." We have surrendered it, not surrendered to it.

After reading the first chapter of this book, a niece cried, "You have opened a wound that I thought had healed."

"It is healed," I replied. "It just doesn't have scar tissue. It isn't calloused." But the mark is permanent.

Tragedies traumatize minds and lives like injuries wound flesh. Scarring from both will heal, diminish and pale with time. But like leaf scars along a plant stem, grief scars need not harm nor disfigure. Once overwhelming, they remain to prove that life has prevailed, has been enriched to foster growth.

The Physician's Review

> The physician's goal is
> the care and cure of the patient,
> "For where there is the love of man,
> there is also love of the Art."
> HIPPOCRATES

Because I had not recorded in my journals the medical procedures noted in the first three chapters of my book, and realizing the fallibility of memory, I invited comments from Stephen's primary physician at Bethesda Naval Hospital. She enthusiastically responded with two detailed, case review tapes which corroborated most of my recollections.

In the following excerpts, however, I also have included personal impressions that will identify her as one among a cadre of physicians who are dedicated to the care and healing of patients, who care deeply about them and their families. I am thankful for Renata Engler who gave unsparingly to our family, who always has spoken to me as a friend.
NRL

My account of Stephen Lantz's last three weeks of life are from the perspective of the caring physician: one not involved with the patient prior to his illness, but who interfaces with his life and is permanently touched and affected by the experience.

After completing a year of general medicine internship at

the Naval Medical Center, Bethesda, Maryland, I had spent two years as a general medical officer in family practice in Spain. I had started an internal medicine residency to expand my skills and understanding of complex diseases. I think that is what motivates many to go into internal medicine, if they can overcome the fear of having to live with always not knowing enough. Such a residency is a painful time, so dramatic in the amount of learning that goes on, so stressful because of the severity of illnesses that must be dealt with every day, and so fatiguing because there is always too much work and never enough time to do it. As the front line doctor, at least in a military residency program, the buck stops with you. When I first met the young midshipman from the Naval Academy at Annapolis upon his arrival at the Naval Hospital, I was approaching the end of my first year in internal medicine residency.

The morning of April 23, 19—, I came in early to make rounds; and by 9:30 my beeper started going off for admissions, one after the other. I don't remember which patient Stephen was, but he was admitted directly to the floor. He was a twenty-one-year-old white male, a very attractive young man despite the obvious severity of his illness. He was really rather beautiful, and I remember thinking he was the ideal officer midshipman that would make the girls swoon. Obviously he had been healthy, physically fit and with a good mind, although that did not function very clearly in view of the tremendous shock of suddenly having to come to the hospital as a patient.

That event clouds people's ability to relate, particularly in the young. Psychiatrists say the adolescent believes himself to be invincible. Even though Stephen no longer was an adolescent, I sensed that he could not grasp the possibility of his mortality or his vulnerability, that an illness had totally, radically changed his life.

As I conducted his history and physical exam, he had what we would call a flat affect: stunned, in shock. I reviewed records from previous encounters with doctors and talked with him to get a complete history [These medical details correlated with my observations and have been omitted here. NRL]

After a brief hospitalization at Andrews Air Force Base Stephen had returned to school and activities, apparently well [by his own assessment]. It was hard to believe that he truly felt well, but easy to understand that he could not admit to feeling unwell. Perhaps his mind could not accept the fact that he was ill. One senses that something is wrong, but wants to get on with life; and illness is a terrible interference with one's plans.

About nine days before coming to the Naval Hospital, Stephen described the onset of right hip and knee pain which he self-treated with analgesics and bedrest. He said the pain cleared until the Saturday prior to admission when he vigorously played tennis in the sun and became somewhat dehydrated. It is noteworthy that he had lost fifteen pounds over the previous four months.

At the time of admission to the NMC, the available medical data indicated a severe generalized disease, almost surely malignant by virtue of its aggressiveness, and multiple organ involvement. Although one hopes this is some type of viral infection that will pass, I knew from the moment I finished Stephen's workup that he was extremely ill, that he would not finish the Naval Academy, and that his life expectancy was extremely brief. Yet I always hope this will be the case that is different; and that although this is obviously a very aggressive cancer, somehow the chemotherapy will work and he will have a remission. I had certainly cared for enough of these patients. If only he could have at least a year or two with his family to adjust his perspective and to set his life in order.

Of course a corner of me always prays for a miracle, particularly for the young; and I feel terribly inadequate that I can't make that miracle happen. Yet, I am playing the role of a world-based physician who works with the tools of medicine to give people the best chance for healing. But I know that medicine alone is nothing; it must be administered with caring, love and the faith of patient and the family, the best medicines of all that support anything we might do.

I tried to talk to Stephen about his family, that they should be called; but I could see he did not understand how much he was going to need them. I explained to him that the disease probably was a malignancy involving many organs—liver, spleen, lymph nodes throughout his body, probably also the bone marrow, which was the cause of the bone pain. He listened with no expression, agreed to call his family, but thought it unnecessary that they come immediately. Knowing the shock all this must be, I did not want to push him too hard that first day. He asked about taking final exams. Could he go to class? When would he be discharged? He did not understand, and I had a very sinking feeling as I left his room.

I notified the surgeons that I needed a lymph node biopsy the following day. It could not wait. It had to be as soon as possible. I presented his case and they agreed. I called Orthopedics. The top priority was to give him some pain relief. Was it just tumor or could something else cause hip pain? They agreed to see him the following day. Even though I had no diagnosis, I knew the Hematology-Oncology Department would be involved, guiding anything I did in terms of chemotherapy.

The first night was hard for Stephen; he had a lot of pain. Next morning he underwent the bone marrow aspirate and biopsy, later the lymph node biopsies. Body temperatures were elevated to 104°F, and we started the cooling blanket in addition to medication for symptomatic relief. His stomach ached, his bones were exquisitely tender—he hurt all over. Again I wondered how this total body pain appeared so rapidly. That day was so eventful for Stephen, yet I could not be with him for all his procedures.

I knew he needed someone, but physicians just do not have enough time. I tucked in the back of my head that his family had to come as soon as possible. I asked him, "Have you talked to your family?"

"Yes."

"Did you tell them to come?"

"No."

I took command. "Your family needs to come. I'll call and talk to them." I could tell from his mother's voice that she knew something was very wrong. They would come.

His fever kept climbing. We drew blood repeatedly for bacterial cultures. He certainly could have been infected. I could not shake the premonition that he would have to be transferred soon to the intensive care unit. His disease was so avaricious, so much of his body appeared to be involved. I had been down this road before. I did not want to think about it yet. We still had to deal in hope. We still had to believe that what we were doing was going to make a difference.

A flurry of activity followed: intravenous hydration; medications to prevent the chemotherapy from doing more harm than necessary (when a lot of cells die, breakdown products such as uric acid can destroy the kidneys); special care for the teeth, gums, rectal areas to minimize mucosal tissue damage and the introduction of infection. (Once the big gun chemotherapy is on board, all the normal immune defenses will be destroyed along with tumor cells, and any healthy bacteria could become killers.) His platelet count plummeted dangerously, placing him at risk for serious bleeding, particularly into the head; we started platelet transfusions. He bruised so easily I restricted the people who could draw blood. We would need his veins for a long time. He must remember to cough and deep breathe to avoid pneumonia.

When I enumerated courses to Stephen, he looked at me with a somewhat hostile stare. I knew he wished everyone would leave him alone so he wouldn't have to be more uncomfortable. He demonstrated considerable denial of the entire situation. He was angry, which was appropriate, but tolerated procedures with grudging good will. All of these needed to be done if he were to have any chance at all. He did not understand. How could I already talk to him about dying, yet death was very near.

By the end of April 24 (Could only two days have passed since Stephen's admission?) the patient complained of persistent hip pain, now left shoulder and arm pain. The steadily increasing, generalized bone pain reflected the massive tumor growth expanding within the bone marrow. The bone marrow biopsy showed the process to be leukemic, but it was not clear what type. Acute lymphocytic leukemia? If that were the type, there was hope he would respond to the chemotherapy. Final slides would not be available until the 25th, the following day, but already plans were being laid for chemotherapy.

So, we thought he had leukemia, lymphoma. His tumor load was difficult to imagine; and even though his fevers might have been due to tumor alone, I had the sickening feeling that an infection was waiting to spring the final trap for Stephen. I told the night Watch to monitor him carefully. At home I told my husband about Stephen. "John David, he's very, very sick. I don't think there is a lot we can do for him; but if we could just buy him some time, some time to feel reasonably well again, to put things in order, and get a perspective on life." Through the centuries, I guess that's what people have always felt so frustrated with, the young who are ill or die suddenly, who have no time to reflect, to make real peace.

April 25, more of the same: fever, hot, cold, pain. Medication brought some relief from the pain. He had developed increasing signs of bleeding in the tissues. T-cell markers from the bone marrow were negative. I guessed that to be good, since a T-cell lymphoma tends to be more malignant. I had elected to begin antibiotics to cover the possibility of a bacterial infection. The handsome features of Stephen's body and face became increasingly deformed by edema in the tissues. Yet I had to pour liters and liters of fluids into his veins in order to assure a minimal urine output from the kidneys. Diuretics relieved some of the fluid overload, but the tissue edema persisted. I placed Stephen on the seriously ill list. I had a foreboding that things were not going well, and that was a way to warn the world that I knew. I called the Lodge to get a room for the patient's parents who were arriving that day.

Several times I talked to the blood bank, explaining the severity of his disease, and the fact that we were in for a long haul and needed lots of blood products. The bank was short. A couple of other leukemics were in the house. They said we would have to do some juggling; we could only give him platelets when there was evidence of bleeding. I wanted to prevent bleeding. Hematology-Oncology supported me and I wheedled extra platelets. If we had waited until he bled into his head, we would have lost the ball game. When the family came, there was the promise of donors.

The night of the 25th: the hospital called me at home. Stephen was complaining of distention of his belly with diffuse pain. His blood pressure had stabilized (for example, his blood pressure did not drop suddenly with sitting up) but there was concern that he had bled into his bowel. They elected to give him medication and observe. He made it through the night.

The 26th: pain in his feet, generalized malaise, still oriented, but the days were taking their toll. Fevers kept ravaging him. He had gained weight, but not good weight, fluid weight. Afternoon: the bone marrow and lymph node biopsies were reviewed by the Hemato-pathology section including Dr.— of National Institute of Health.

From the note I sensed that no one was absolutely clear as to his tumor type. The decision was by committee. All lymphoid tissue was infiltrated massively. The clinical aggressiveness suggested a lymphoblastic lymphoma or a poorly differentiated diffuse lymphoma. I sensed that they were not sure, that this was such an undifferentiated tumor and so aggressive that diagnosis was a stab in the dark. Bottom line, it was a bad tumor. I felt helpless that I did not have the knowledge to critically review those slides. But differentiating between histiocytic leukemia, acute lymphoblastic leukemia with lymphomatous changes, or lymphoma in a leukemic phase are subtleties that were above my head; and, I guessed, above a lot of other heads.

They decided to recommend treatment for acute leukemia because of the aggressiveness of the clinical course. I prayed the choices were correct. Certainly we were using shotgun medicines: Cytoxin, high dose Prednisone, Vincristine, Adriamycin—the big guns day one and day eight, the Prednisone for twenty-eight days. I would give the therapy; and, dear God, let it work, or at least have it buy us some time.

I was depressed about Stephen because, unlike many patients, I couldn't touch him. I tried to talk to him honestly, to open a door to an awareness of what was happening; but he was still in shock. His family were wonderful, warm, supportive; I liked them. They appeared to be good people who cared and obviously loved him dearly. I was grateful that they were there; at least he had someone with him who loved him and whom he loved. That is a blessing not all patients have. I knew his family understood how serious it was. They knew what he had been like when he was well, how radical the change. I wished I could give them more hope. They knew we were doing our best. Yet, we were caught in the eye of the storm. We followed our steps and that was all we could do.

April 27: we drew blood on the family members to give him platelets he would not chew up so fast. Now he needed morphine to relieve pain, as well as oxygen. His lungs were in trouble, that dread complication, adult respiratory distress syndrome. At this time I had a tremendous sense of the inevitable, knowing that the ICU would soon become our work place for him. The Ward nurses complained, "We can't handle this. We're running an ICU on the Ward. He needs to be downstairs." I agreed, but beds were short; and we had to do our best until we had no other choice.

I knew we were giving him too many fluids, but we had to give them or his kidneys would shut down from the tumor chemotherapy. He had gained fourteen pounds in two days; and it was fluid in his belly, fluid in his legs and rales in his lungs. Pneumonia or fluid? His electrolytes showed that we were keeping up reasonably well, but I knew it was only temporary. If only enough of the tumor would die so his healthy tissues could regroup, but he became short of breath and his hematocrit [red cell count] declined. We had thought his belly enlargement was due to fluid, but the ultrasound showed none. Dear God, was this all tumor and inflammation? Had his whole spleen been replaced by tumor?

On the 27th I went home with an overwhelming sense of failure. The Watch called me at midnight. Stephen seemed to have progressed to acute respiratory distress with pulmonary edema. He made it through the night, but was now up to 50% oxygen supplemation. [Atmospheric air is 21% oxygen by volume.] It was only a question of time before we had to move him to the ICU.

April 28: at 3:00 a.m. there were symptoms and signs of heart failure. They had placed a nasogastric tube in the stomach to prevent vomiting, but the patient pulled it out. I knew frustration and despair must be enveloping his mind and spirit. He wished the I.V.'s, the blood drawing would all go away, but we couldn't stop now. We wrote *clinically improved* because the numbers were balanced; in actual fact, I did not know if we were getting anywhere. His liver did not seem to have decreased in size, and that melting away of lymph nodes that we always like to see had not happened. On the 28th I wrote a long summary note: He was better in the morning, with decreased shortness of breath. The efforts of vigorous diuresis had helped. His chest sounded clearer, but he had an increasing risk for severe bleeding. We were doing our best. I summarized the problems, the list getting ever longer.

The 29th: we continued chemotherapy and platelet transfusions. Continued belly symptoms worried us. General Surgery followed him with us; but if he needed surgery, I knew he could not survive.

April 30: more of the same. Things had stabilized for awhile, but he looked so ill. The Hematology-Oncology note was brief: *continued support.* Yes, we would continue support. More abdominal pain, more fever the night of the 30th. His white blood count hit 450. [Normal is greater than 3500.] All those important cells we need to protect us from our environment were depleted, leaving Stephen's body defenseless. He was placed in isolation to decrease his exposure to pathogens, but how could we isolate him from himself?

May 1: more abdominal pain, but chest was clear. On that morning, Stephen's temperature spiked to 103°F and he had markedly increased pain in the right upper quadrant of his abdomen. He was in respiratory distress. Culture after culture was taken from blood, sputum, urine, I.V. sites: the massive search for infection continued.

May 2: the chest x-ray now showed a diffuse intra-alveolar pattern of infiltrates, bilaterally. Tumor? Tumor destruction? Pneumonia? Infection due to immuno-suppression? The eternal unknowns are always the focus of rounds. A Swan-Ganz catheter placed into the pulmonary artery, via the veins and right side of the heart, would facilitate the fluid management, but required intensive care unit services. There were moments when he seemed a little better; but certainly in the context of the overall picture, he was gravely ill with no signs of improvement. On the morning of May 2, he again became increasingly tachypneic [accelerated heart rate] and short of breath, with a temperature spike to 104°F, evidence of heart failure, and deteriorating blood gases.

Stephen was transferred to the ICU and started on four antibiotics to deal with anything infectious. Cardiothoracic Surgery was called for an emergency open lung biopsy. There was some resistance to the biopsy because of the patient's instability, but I rallied support and it was performed with no difficulty. Chest tube was in place and suctioning. So many tubes. I could see from his face he was tired of it all.

I sat down with the family to explain: no bacteria evident, no fungal elements, no pneumocysts. It was so hard. He was so young, had been so perfect. Now his body was ravaged by disease. I did not touch her closely, but I saw the agony of his sister. Such a young girl. And his fiancée who had lost her handsome prince to this horrible, strange attacker of a disease.

I knew Stephen would die, but I kept trying. We all kept trying. We had to in honor of his youth, in honor of his potential, in honor of hope. As I looked at Stephen's body that now was ugly and distorted, I was reminded that perhaps we take physical reality too seriously. If Stephen died, he wouldn't be dead; he would still live, free. The tragedy is that we believe that; we do not know it. This material world is so real and holds us with agony. One good thing about work: it was all-consuming. The days left no time to think for too long. Reflections came later, in the wake of death. At the time, in the heat of battle, I did not want time to reflect.

May 3: continued antibiotics, respiratory support, blood products, fluid management, 70% oxygen. We still hoped for something dramatic from the chemotherapy.

Because of increased difficulty in breathing, Stephen was robbed of another freedom on the morning of May 4: an endotracheal tube was placed to help him breathe, and now he could not talk. Respiratory distress was alleviated.

So much had happened since his arrival on the 23rd of April. I was worried about his nutrition. Malnourished patients cannot heal as well; they do not tolerate chemotherapy as well. In the midst of Stephen's complexities, hyperalimentation [feeding through the vein] was the last thing on anyone's mind. Now I tackled it as a formal problem. Since I was afraid to place a central feeding line because of the risks of infection, we tried nasogastric feeding with a blenderized diet, one calorie milliliter; but his bowels were inflamed and I doubted that he would tolerate the feedings.

Response to the chemotherapy was far from impressive. The possibility that the tumor was extraordinarily refractory, or the diagnosis in error, was reconsidered. If, within the next couple of days, we could stabilize Stephen without reversal of his organomegaly [enlargement of the liver, spleen, etc.] we could consider adding other chemotherapy.

Because his white blood count was close to zero, white blood cell transfusions were recommended. I was not excited about them because his lungs already were so fragile, and one complication with white cell transfusions is clogging of the lungs because of clotting of the cells. Family members could donate and everyone felt the same: we had to try. The question of infection continued, but nothing had been found. Again, my sinking feeling was that this was all tumor and we were chasing our tails.

On the 4th I wrote an addendum: It still appeared most probable that the primary disease was a lymphoid precursor malignancy, leukemic or lymphomatous. As long as this was true, the chemotherapy should provide the optimum benefit; but the tumor load may be too great. On careful review, his lung biopsy showed myelocytic cells. As suspected, tumor was in his lung tissue. I discussed the patient at length with the family. On the possibility that part of the respiratory compromise was based on imposed infection, we proceeded with white cell transfusions.

The roulette of antibiotics continued, token changes with each fever spike; but I had an overwhelming sense of futility that his fever primarily was due to tumor, and that changing the antibiotics was an exercise in intellectualism. I pressed for consideration of a different chemotherapeutic regimen.

May 7: another bone marrow was performed but an aspirate was not obtainable. Touch preps showed persistent, bizarre, malignant, mononuclear cells. Continued evidence of bleeding, but it was low grade and all we could do was continue what we were doing. The feedings were not going well. His nutrition was abysmal. He was starving. How could his tissues respond or recoup? I pushed to feed him, for I felt it was his only chance; yet I did not want to hurt him by causing him to aspirate. Catch 22's continued, and I gave his chemotherapy.

Problem 10, Stephen's mental status. Now that he was in the ICU, it was harder for me to relate to him. He was appropriately depressed. He understood the need for what we were doing, but he needed more support than I thought we could give. I explained each new step we were doing, but I saw in his eyes that he was angry and hopeless. I think he knew. I wished we could talk about death and dying, of hope beyond this life. I thought again of all the work that Kübler-Ross has done, and how important it is that one dies surrounded by love and with an acceptance of what is to come. In our highly charged medical environments, dying is so hard to do; yet all I could do was pray for him because I was not let in. I could only reach out to his family and hoped they could do what I could not.

We prescribed medications to relieve suffering. I did not like doping him but I thought it better if, for at least part of the time, we gave him escape. It is so hard to sleep or rest in the ICU.

May 8: I thought his respiratory status a little better. I deluded myself that perhaps it was the new chemotherapy. Increased gastrointestinal bleeding and low platelet counts forced us to stop some antibiotics.

May 9: Dr. S— and I reviewed Stephen's case. The tumor load at the onset of this second therapy was so extreme and his multisystem disease so severe that the chance of dramatic improvement was extremely slim. Severity of Stephen's situation lead us to a combined and agreed upon decision to vigorously treat his problems but not to include cardio-pulmonary resuscitation. The consequences of CPR would be so disastrous that it would not have been justifiable to continue.

This was the realization that Stephen was dying. For the family, I think, it was clear now. I thought Stephen too sick to understand fully, although I think he must have known. I found I could not talk to him about it; I talked only about specifics: his breathing; where did it hurt? what could we do to make him feel more comfortable? Rather, I talked to his family and hoped they could communicate for me our support and care, and a sense of what was developing. Whenever I looked at Stephen, I thought of all the young who die before they should; and I felt the same mixture of anger and frustration that his parents, his sister, his fiancée and he must have felt.

May 10: Dr. S— wrote, "Special studies are back on the malignant cells, electron-microscopic studies definitely suggest a lympoid origin to the tumor, most probably a histiocytic lymphoma. This type of tumor usually responds to the vigorous chemotherapy we've given; but a lack of response is not unheard of." I thought his nodes were down. I felt as if there had been some response. I was encouraged; but he was so sick, that I did not hang my hopes too high.

The 11th and 12th of May: we continued vigorous support systems and surveillance. The Watch doctor commented that the patient appeared severely depressed. Inside, my little person laughed a little at the triteness of that comment.

During early morning of the 13th, Stephen's condition deteriorated. I thought he was in septic shock [overwhelming infection] but I also believed his tissues to be consumed by tumor. By evening I went home, exhausted. Dr. C— was on that night. He is very good, and I knew he would keep tabs. I did not want to be there when Stephen died. I guess that was a coward's response. There was nothing more I could do, and I knew that. Dr. C— called me at midnight that Stephen was dead.

The next day was my birthday. At the time I forgot that it was, as the day dealt with all the things that need to be done after one dies. In our society it is far more difficult to die than to be born. We had permission for an autopsy, but so much had to be done by the family. And families are not left to their grief, but must deal with the bureaucratic demands associated with death.

Stephen was at one of the most magical times in one's life, the completion of college and looking to the future as an adult who will function with commitment. The phrase *severe mercy* [from a book by Sheldon Vanauken] has meaning that may be able to be tranlated into his family's experience with his death.

It is said that the young who die are spared the agonies of losses, disillusionment and pains that people must deal with as they grow older, yet a severe mercy. Still with the blush of innocence, hope and idealism, Stephen died never having killed another human being. As one of the military, how long would our world have spared him that atrocious reality? He never would have to suffer the pain of losing his own child with all the unexpressed potential, again a severe mercy for all the anguish that subsequently was suffered by his family.

That he loved them, and was loved, was a precious gift. Stephen died in his springtime, a beautiful time of life to witness, to be cherished with its memory.

end of file

Notes

A *Page 12*—Elizabeth Ann Seton, mother of a family of five that included two Navy sons, devoted her life to serving people during the early nineteenth century and founded the first parochial school and religious order for women in the United States. A hundred years and more after her death, prayers of intercession to Mother Seton resulted in miraculous cures of terminal patients. The Roman Catholic Church elevated her to sainthood in 1975 because of these miracles and for her indomitable faith and good works.
   Hindman, Jane F. *Elizabeth Ann Seton: Mother, Teacher, Saint for Our Time.* New York: Arena Lettres, 1976.

B *Page 14*—Pheresis is a mechanical process in which whole blood is extracted from a donor, centrifically separated into components (for example, plasma, platelets, red and white cells) and collected according to patient need. The remaining elements are returned to the donor.

C *Page 29*—"Joy in the Morning" was a meditation that inspired me to examine the paradox of joy coexisting with the anguish of the moment.

D *Page 56*—Gold stars earned each semester for academic excellence are worn on midshipman uniform collars.

E *Page 61*—"Youth of the Year" is a National Exchange Club Award presented to high school seniors who demonstrate leadership, scholarship and citizenship.

F *Page 103*—While a high school senior of the class of 1976, Stephen headed a student committee that commemorated the nation's Bicentennial by constructing a 9 by 15 foot Bennington flag, afterward on display in the school media center.

G *Page 105*—Although sirens had wailed, neither we nor others in the immediate area with whom I spoke had heard them or the Valkyrie-like shrieks that announce a tornado. I wondered if diminished sound was due to our position near the silent vacuum of the storm center.

H *Page 109*—Formerly, the Coca Cola Company awarded a carton of Coke to anyone holding this rare, unfortunate hand with no card above a nine.

I *Page 126*—A suspicious explosion aboard the *USS Maine* in the Cuban harbor in 1898 sank the ship, killed 260 and precipitated the Spanish-American War. Recovered later, the foremast was erected at the Naval Academy in 1913; the mainmast is in Arlington National Cemetery.

J *Page 138*—Care-giving refers to the Stephen Ministries, an interdenominational organization founded by Dr. Kenneth C. Haugk, pastor and clinical psychologist, and based in St. Louis, Missouri. Through a holistic, educational approach, the Stephen Series trains and equips lay persons with specific skills in distinctively Christian-focused caring and relating to those who hurt, while promoting growth in its trainees through heightened awareness of the concepts of caring ministry as a way of life.

References

1 Thomas, Captain William N., Chaplain USNA 1933-1945. From *Reef Points, The Annual Handbook of the Brigade of Midshipmen.* Annapolis, Maryland: United States Naval Academy, 1976-1977.

2 Churchill, Sarah. *A Thread in the Tapestry.* New York: Dodd, Mead and Company, 1967.

3 Richard Rodgers and Oscar Hammerstein II. "You'll Never Walk Alone." Copyright© 1945 Williamson Music, Inc. Copyright Renewed. Sole Selling Agent, T. B. Harms Company, c/o The Welk Music Group, Santa Monica, California 90401. International Copyright Secured. All Rights Reserved. Made in U.S.A.

4 Ramsey Ehrlich, Judith. "Make Today Count" *Family Circle* January, 1977. Reprinted with permission from the February 1978 *Reader's Digest* and Ms. Ramsey Ehrlich.

5 Moody, Raymond A., Jr. *Life After Life.* St. Simon's Island, Georgia: Mockingbird Books, 1976.

6 Carr, Emily. *House of All Sorts.* Richmond Hill, Ontario: Irwin Publishing, Inc., 1944. Used by permission of the publishers.

7 Kim Gannon, lyrics and Walter Kent, music. "I'll Be Home for Christmas" Los Angeles, California: Gannon & Kent Music Co., Inc., © 1943.

8 Ogburn, Charlton, Jr. *The Winter Beach.* New York: Morrow Quill Paperbacks, 1979.

9 Gibran, Kahlil. *The Prophet,* "On Death". Reprinted by permission of Alfred A. Knopf, Inc. Copyright 1923 by Kahlil Gibran and renewed 1951 by Administrators C. T. A. of the Kahlil Gibran Estate and Mary G. Gibran.

10 O'Morrison, Kevin. "Ladyhouse Blues". New York: William Morris Agency, 1976. Used with permission from Mr. O'Morrison.

11 Jaffe, Dennis T., Ph.D. *Healing from Within*. New York: Alfred A. Knopf, 1980.

12 Edsall, Margaret Horton *A Place Called The Yard: Guide to the United States Naval Academy.* Davidsonville, Maryland: The Douglas W. Edsall Company, © 1976.

13 Gibran, Kahlil, *The Prophet,* "On Children" Reprinted by permission of Alfred A. Knopf, Inc. Copyright 1923 by Kahlil Gibran and renewed 1951 by Administrators C. T. A. of the Kahlil Gibran Estate and Mary G. Gibran.

14 Thompson, Ernest. "On Golden Pond". New York: Dodd, Mead & Company, Inc. © 1979.

In May, 1987, 2,000 copies of this book were printed and bound by Ihling Bros. Everard Co. in Kalamazoo, Michigan. The body type is 11 point Optima and the titles are Goudy Cursive in various sizes.

ABOUT THE AUTHOR

Norma Lantz began her careers as a secondary teacher of languages and science, then directed teen and young adult programs for the YWCA. Marriage added homemaking, tutoring, adult education instruction and management of the family rental properties. An active volunteer, she has led and participated in Scouting, her church, the Red Cross, community theaters and community access TV production. Hobbies include reading, gardening, crafts, travel and walking. A free-lance writer, her bimonthly herb column appears in a homemakers' newsletter.

ORDER   AFTER STEPHEN: From Hurting to Healed
by Norma R. Lantz

FROM   -aP
—ana Publishing
Post Office Box 625
Kalamazoo, Michigan 49005

RETAIL PRICE $9.95 plus $1.55 postage
and handling. Michigan addresses add
$.40 sales tax.